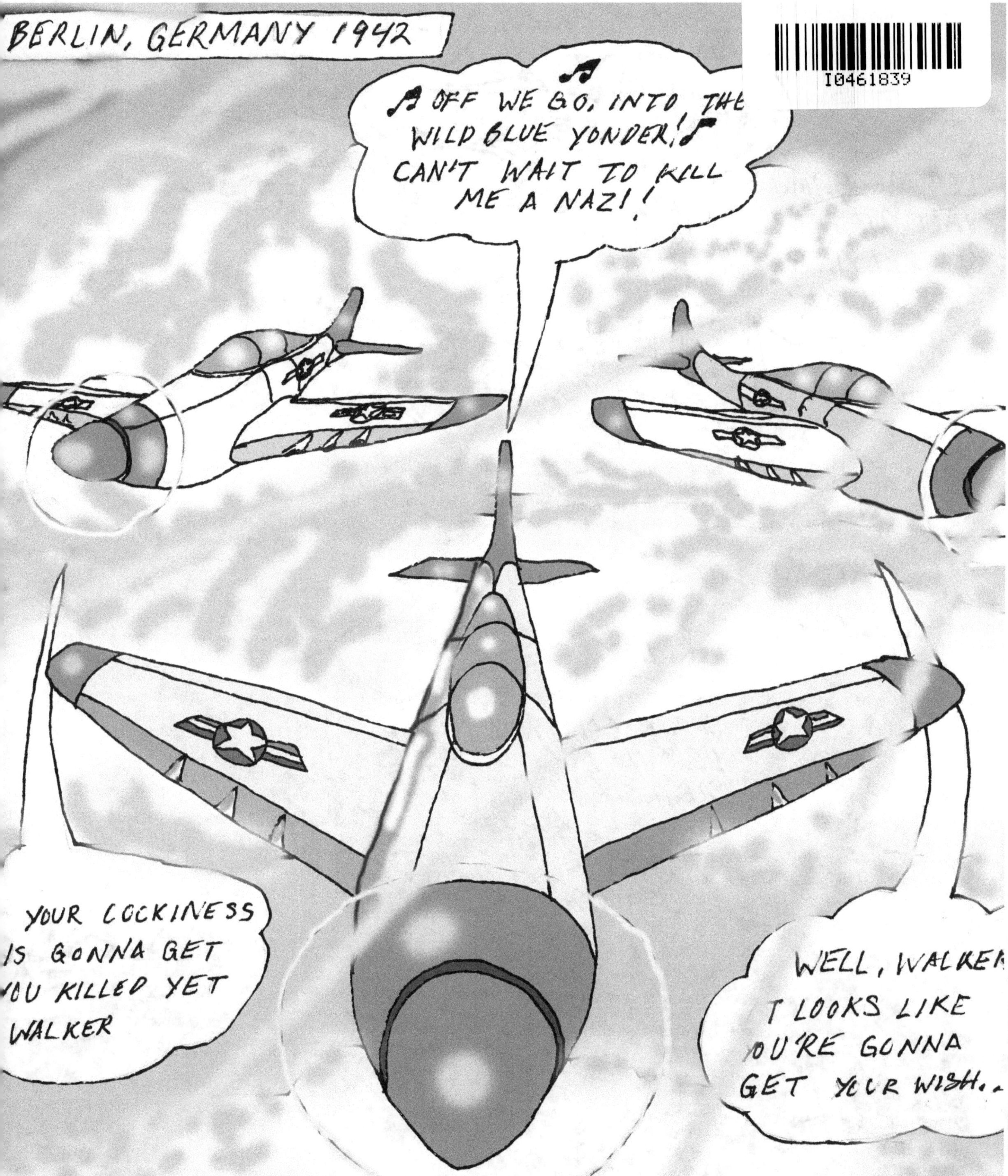
BERLIN, GERMANY 1942
♫ OFF WE GO, INTO THE WILD BLUE YONDER! ♫ CAN'T WAIT TO KILL ME A NAZI!
YOUR COCKINESS IS GONNA GET OU KILLED YET WALKER
WELL, WALKE T LOOKS LIKE OU'RE GONNA GET YOUR WISH...

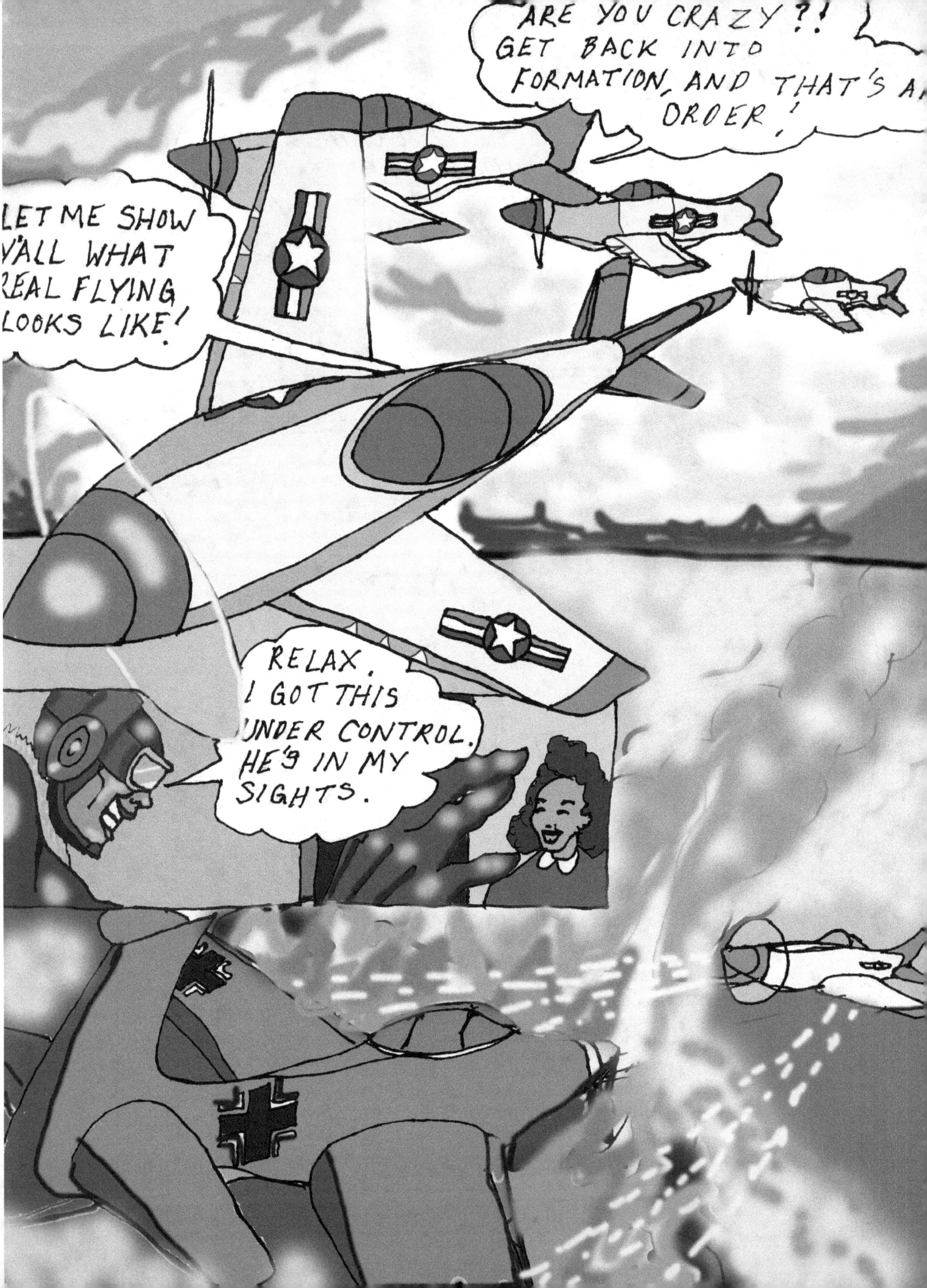
ARE YOU CRAZY?! GET BACK INTO FORMATION, AND THAT'S A ORDER!
LET ME SHOW Y'ALL WHAT REAL FLYING LOOKS LIKE!
RELAX. I GOT THIS UNDER CONTROL. HE'S IN MY SIGHTS.

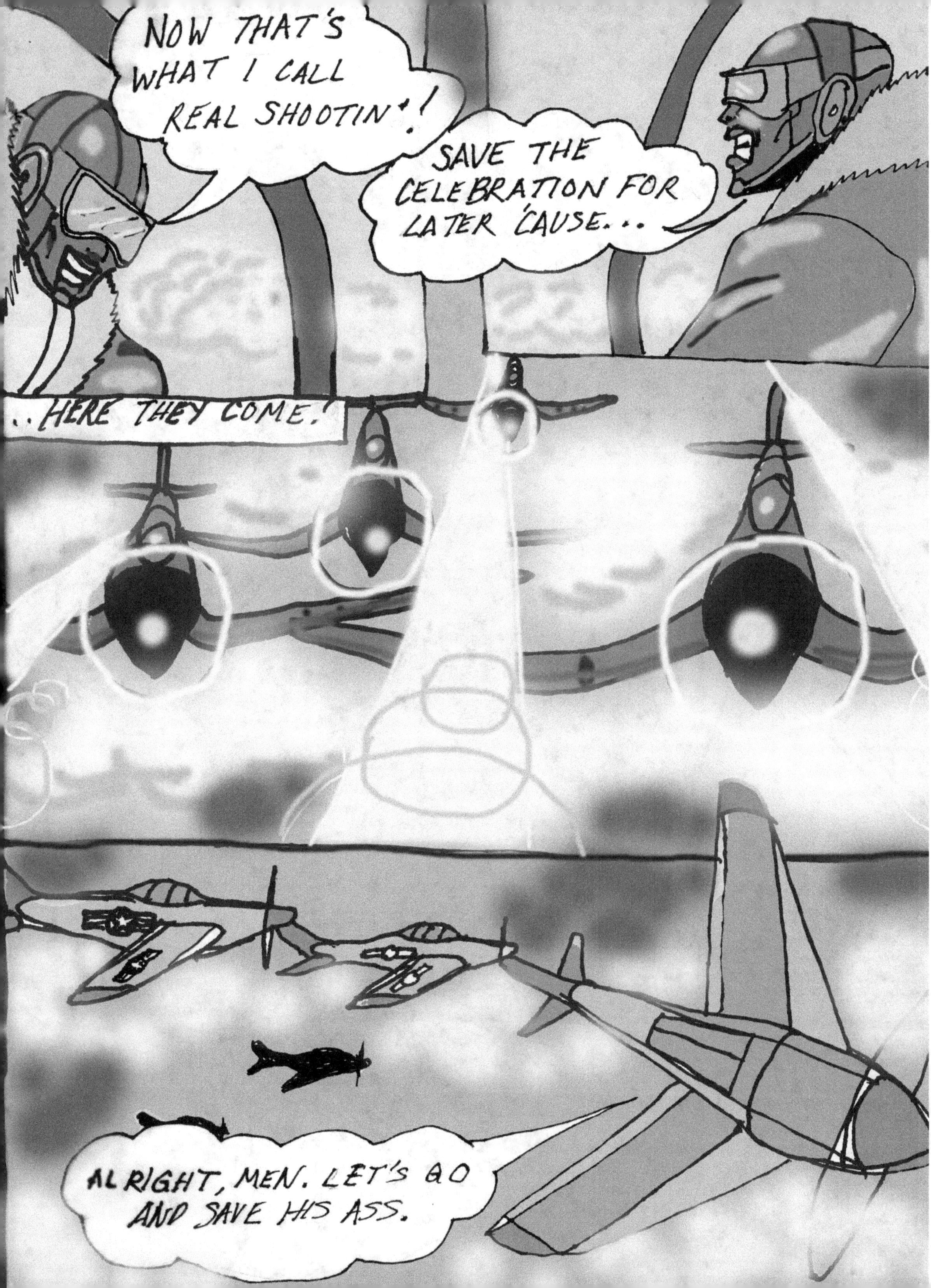
NOW THAT'S WHAT I CALL REAL SHOOTIN'!
SAVE THE CELEBRATION FOR LATER 'CAUSE...
..HERE THEY COME!
ALRIGHT, MEN. LET'S GO AND SAVE HIS ASS.

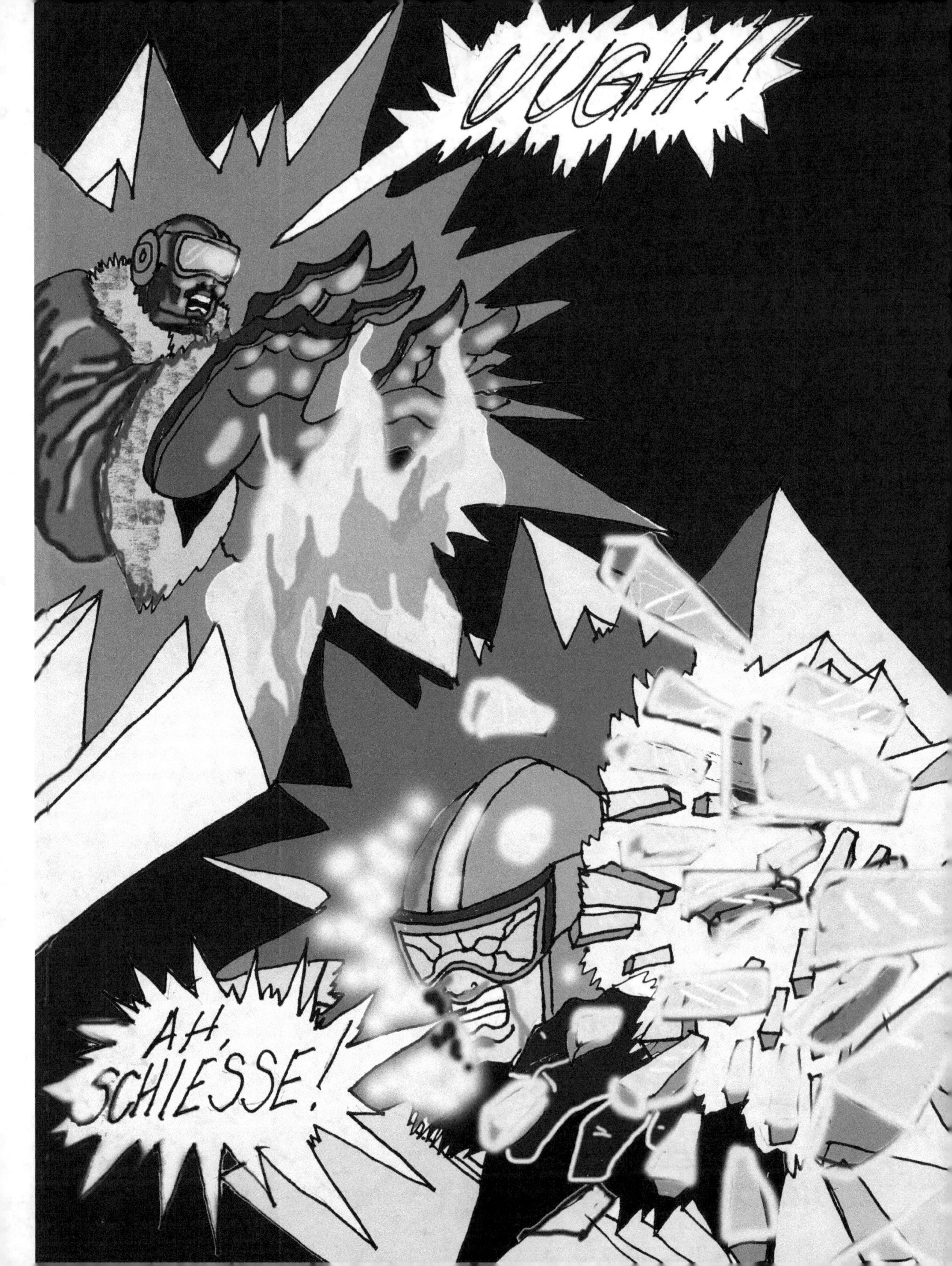
UUGH!!
AH, SCHIESSE!

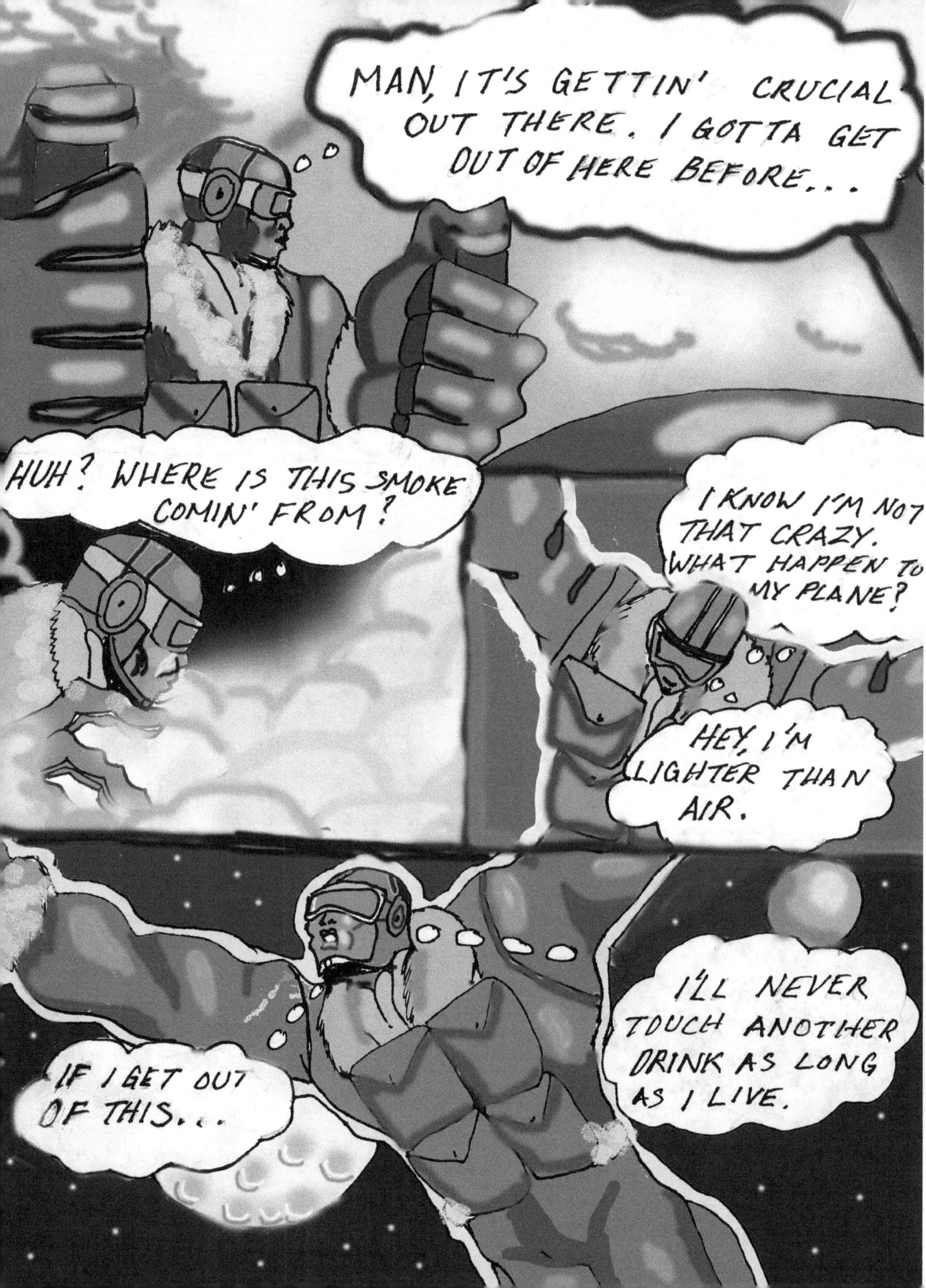
MAN, IT'S GETTIN' CRUCIAL OUT THERE. I GOTTA GET OUT OF HERE BEFORE...
HUH? WHERE IS THIS SMOKE COMIN' FROM?
I KNOW I'M NOT THAT CRAZY. WHAT HAPPEN TO MY PLANE?
HEY, I'M LIGHTER THAN AIR.
IF I GET OUT OF THIS...
I'LL NEVER TOUCH ANOTHER DRINK AS LONG AS I LIVE.

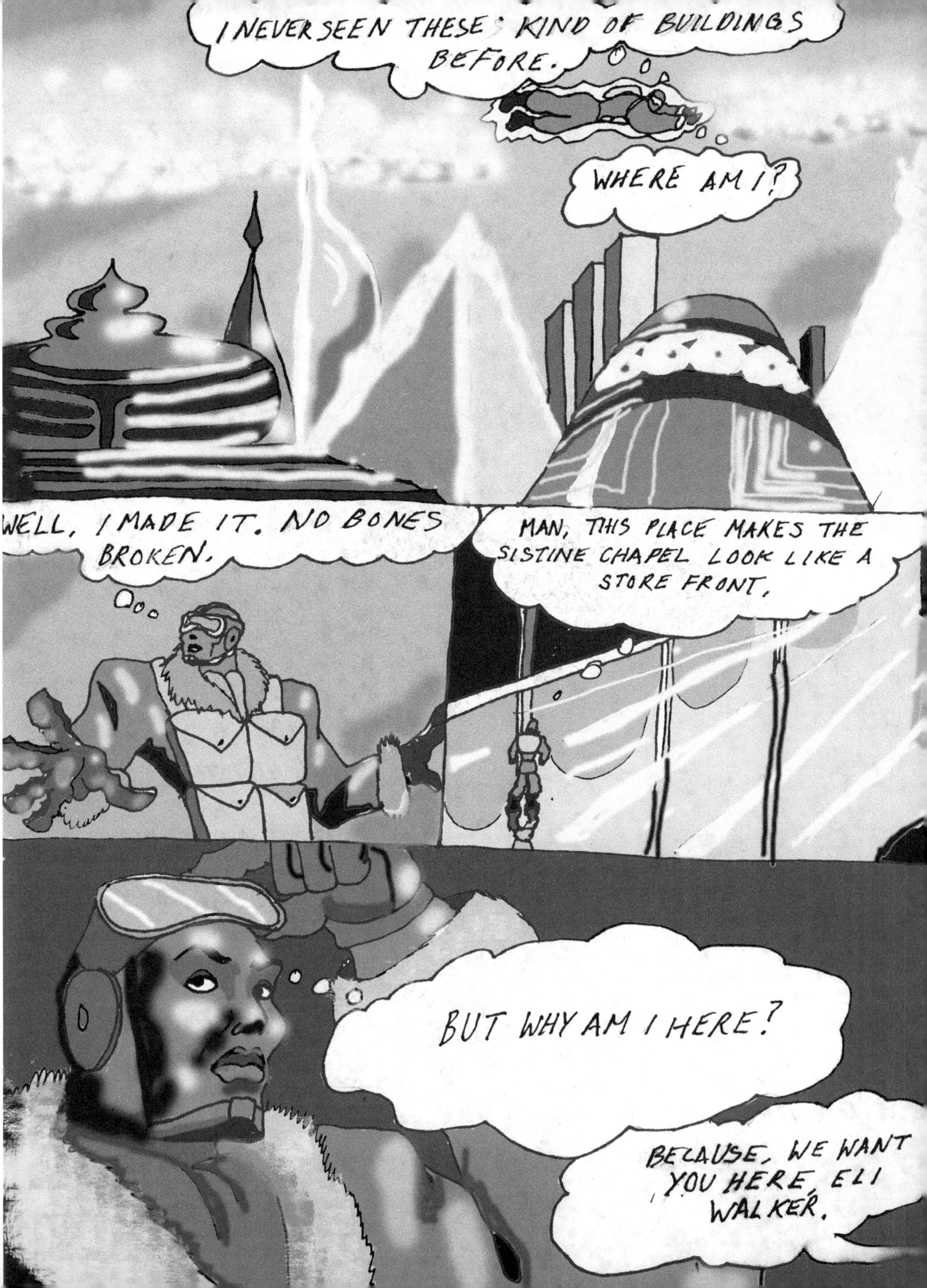
I NEVER SEEN THESE KIND OF BUILDINGS BEFORE.
WHERE AM I?
WELL, I MADE IT. NO BONES BROKEN.
MAN, THIS PLACE MAKES THE SISTINE CHAPEL LOOK LIKE A STORE FRONT.
BUT WHY AM I HERE?
BECAUSE, WE WANT YOU HERE, ELI WALKER.

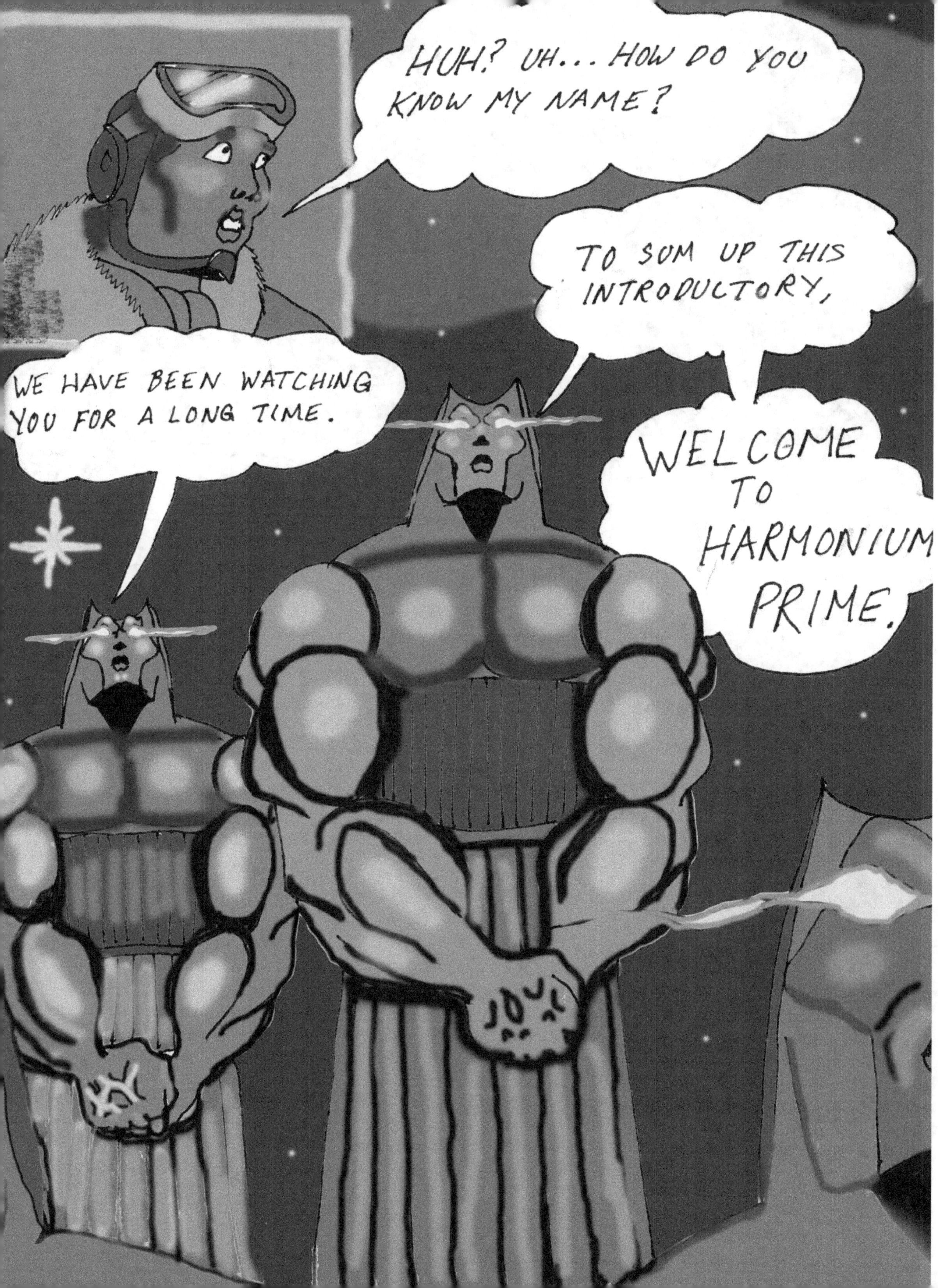
HUH? UH... HOW DO YOU KNOW MY NAME?
WE HAVE BEEN WATCHING YOU FOR A LONG TIME.
TO SUM UP THIS INTRODUCTORY,
WELCOME TO HARMONIUM PRIME.

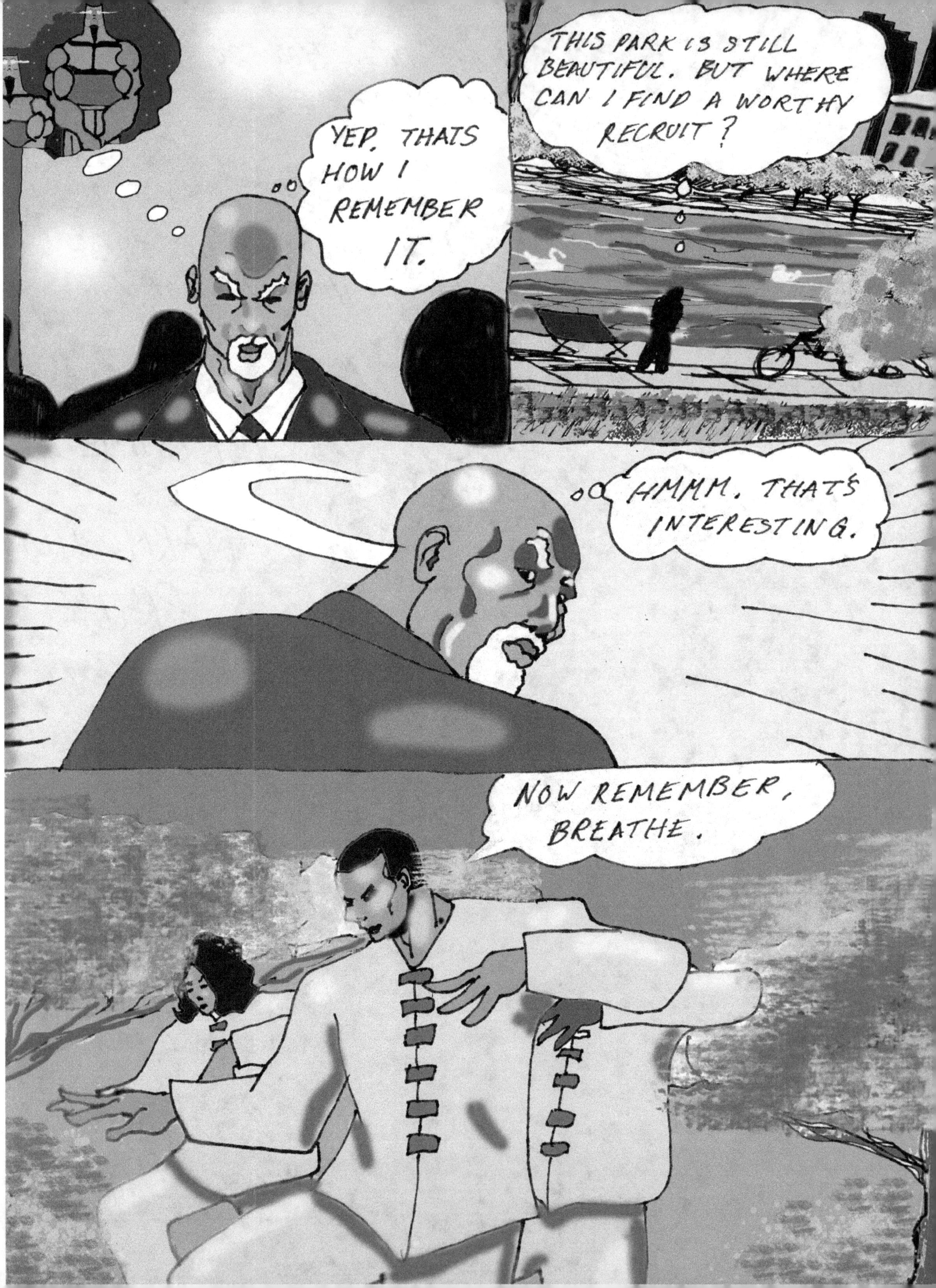
YEP. THATS HOW I REMEMBER IT.
THIS PARK IS STILL BEAUTIFUL. BUT WHERE CAN I FIND A WORTHY RECRUIT?
HMMM. THAT'S INTERESTING.
NOW REMEMBER, BREATHE.

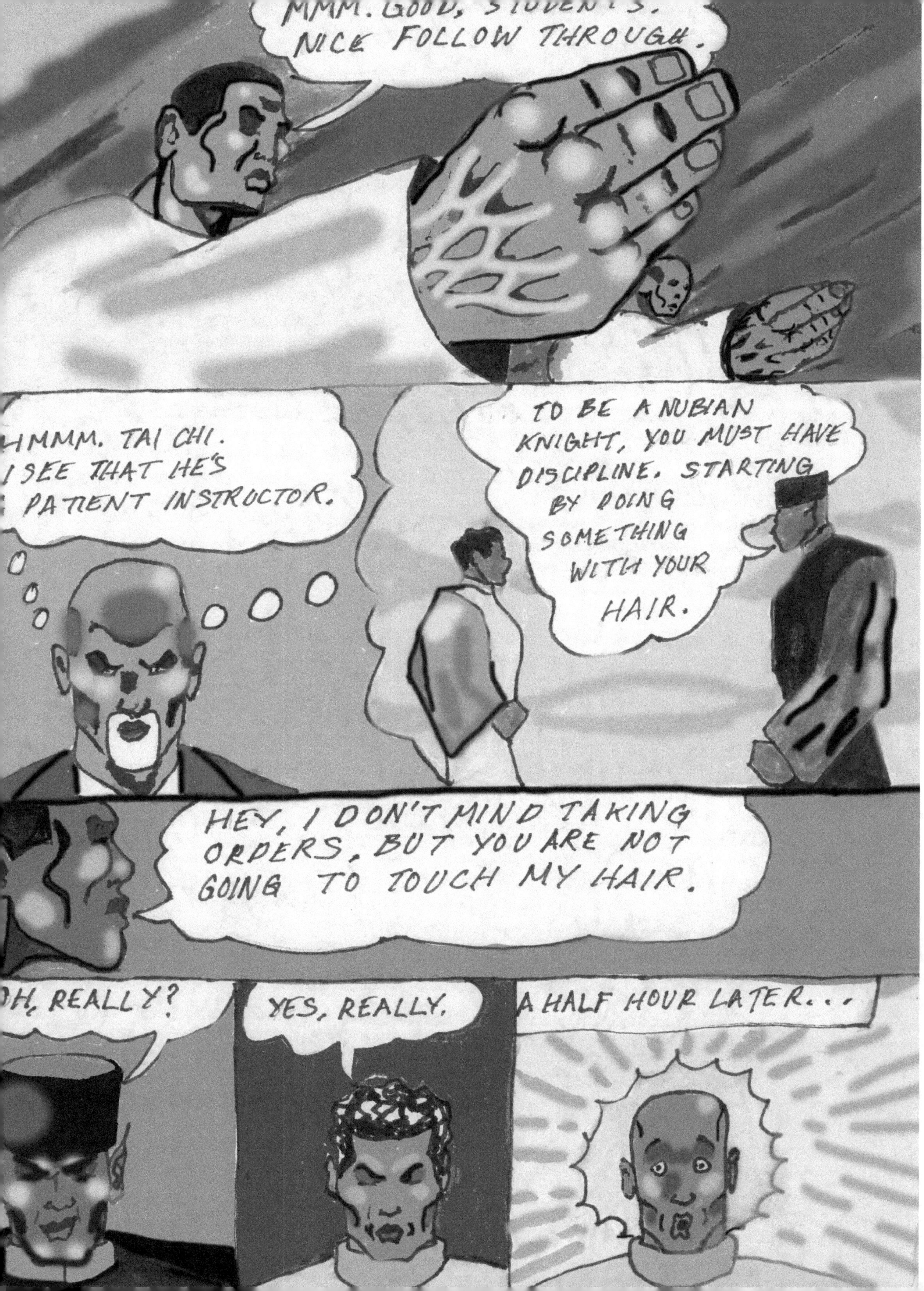
MMM. GOOD, STUDENTS. NICE FOLLOW THROUGH.
HMMM. TAI CHI. I SEE THAT HE'S PATIENT INSTRUCTOR.
TO BE A NUBIAN KNIGHT, YOU MUST HAVE DISCIPLINE. STARTING BY DOING SOMETHING WITH YOUR HAIR.
HEY, I DON'T MIND TAKING ORDERS, BUT YOU ARE NOT GOING TO TOUCH MY HAIR.
OH, REALLY?
YES, REALLY.
A HALF HOUR LATER...

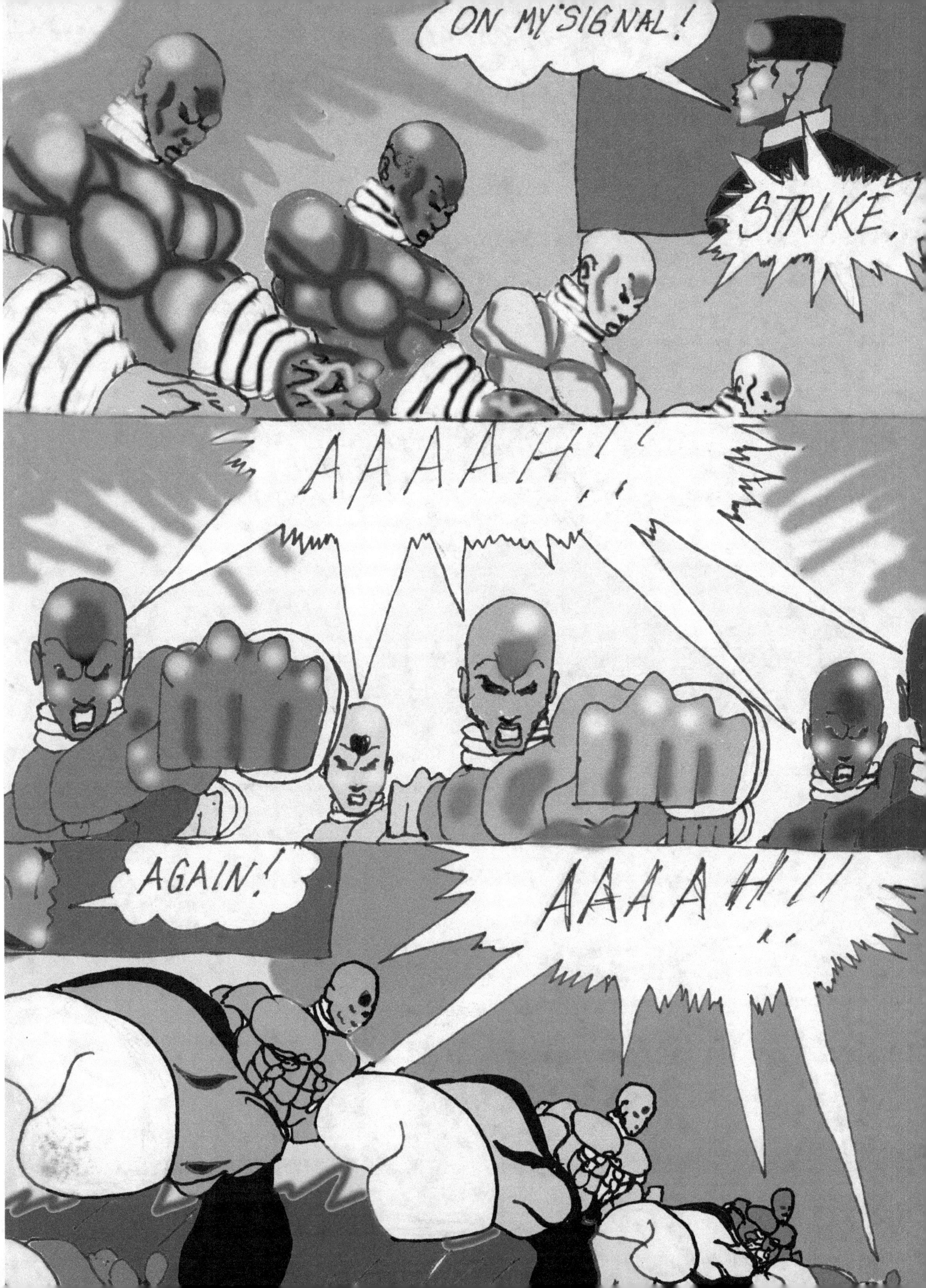
ON MY SIGNAL!
STRIKE!
AAAAH!!
AGAIN!
AAAAH!!

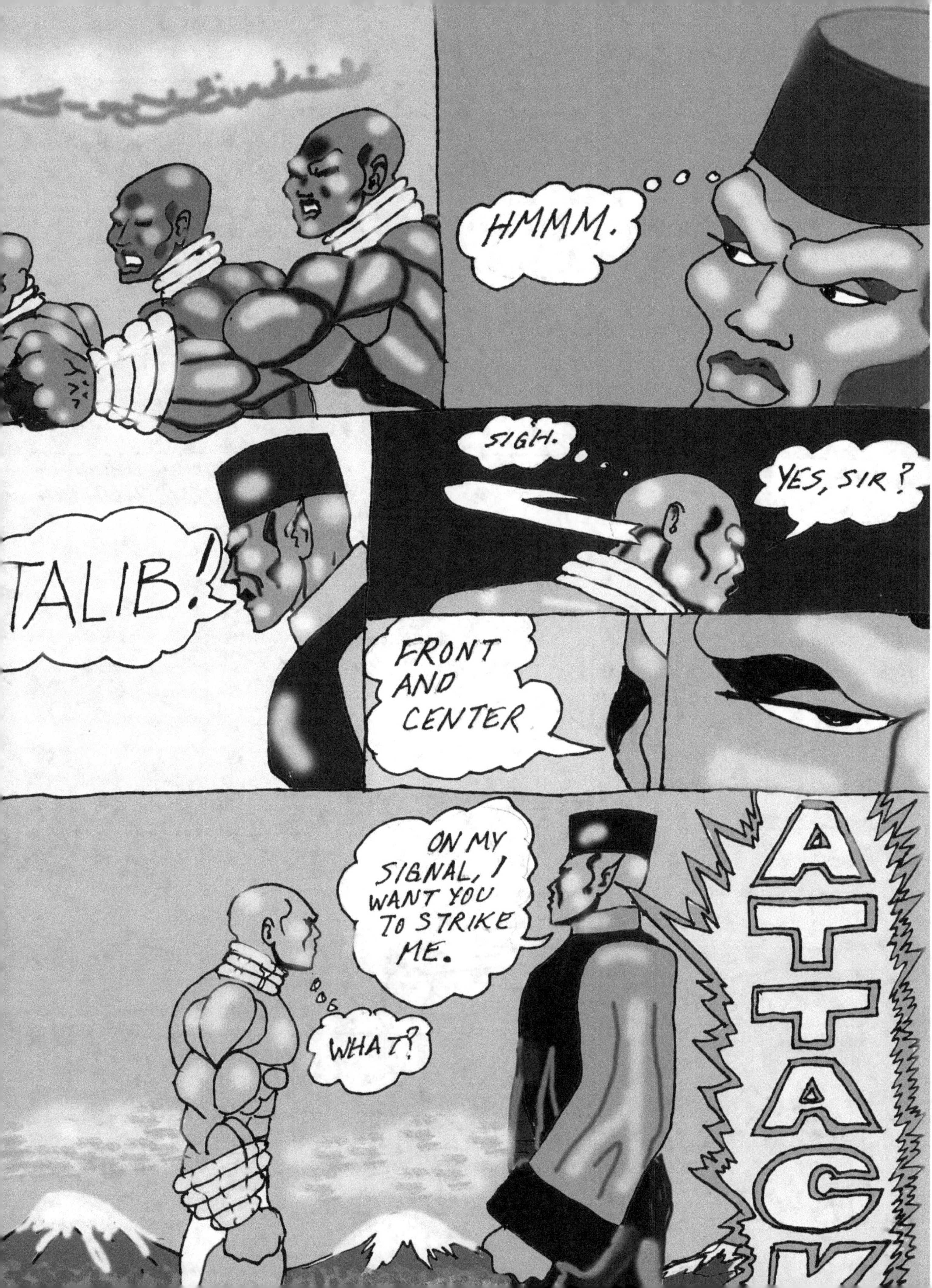
HMMM.
TALIB!
SIGH.
YES, SIR?
FRONT AND CENTER
ON MY SIGNAL, I WANT YOU TO STRIKE ME.
WHAT?
ATTAC

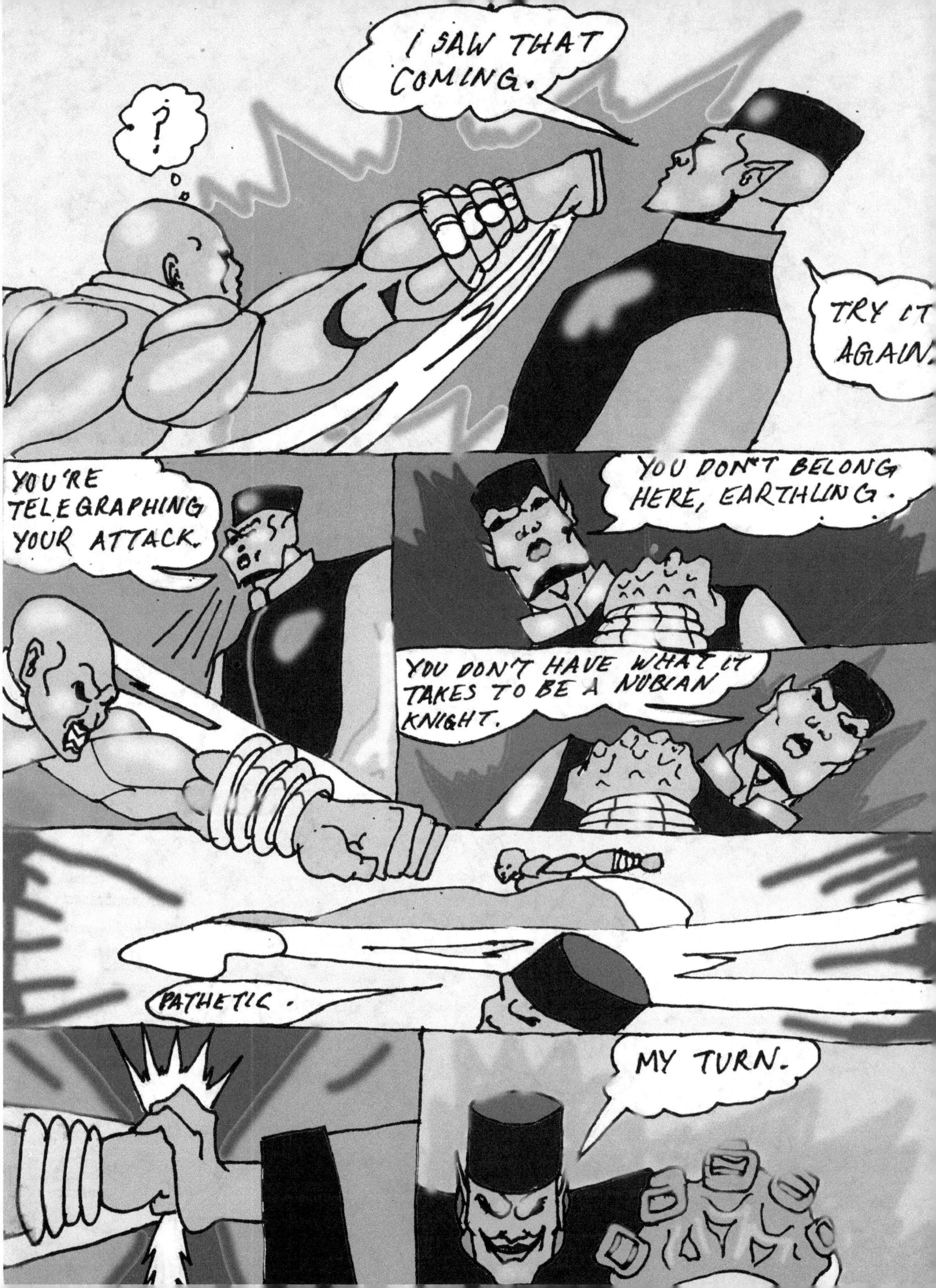
?
I SAW THAT COMING.
TRY IT AGAIN.
YOU'RE TELEGRAPHING YOUR ATTACK.
YOU DON'T BELONG HERE, EARTHLING.
YOU DON'T HAVE WHAT IT TAKES TO BE A NUBIAN KNIGHT.
PATHETIC.
MY TURN.

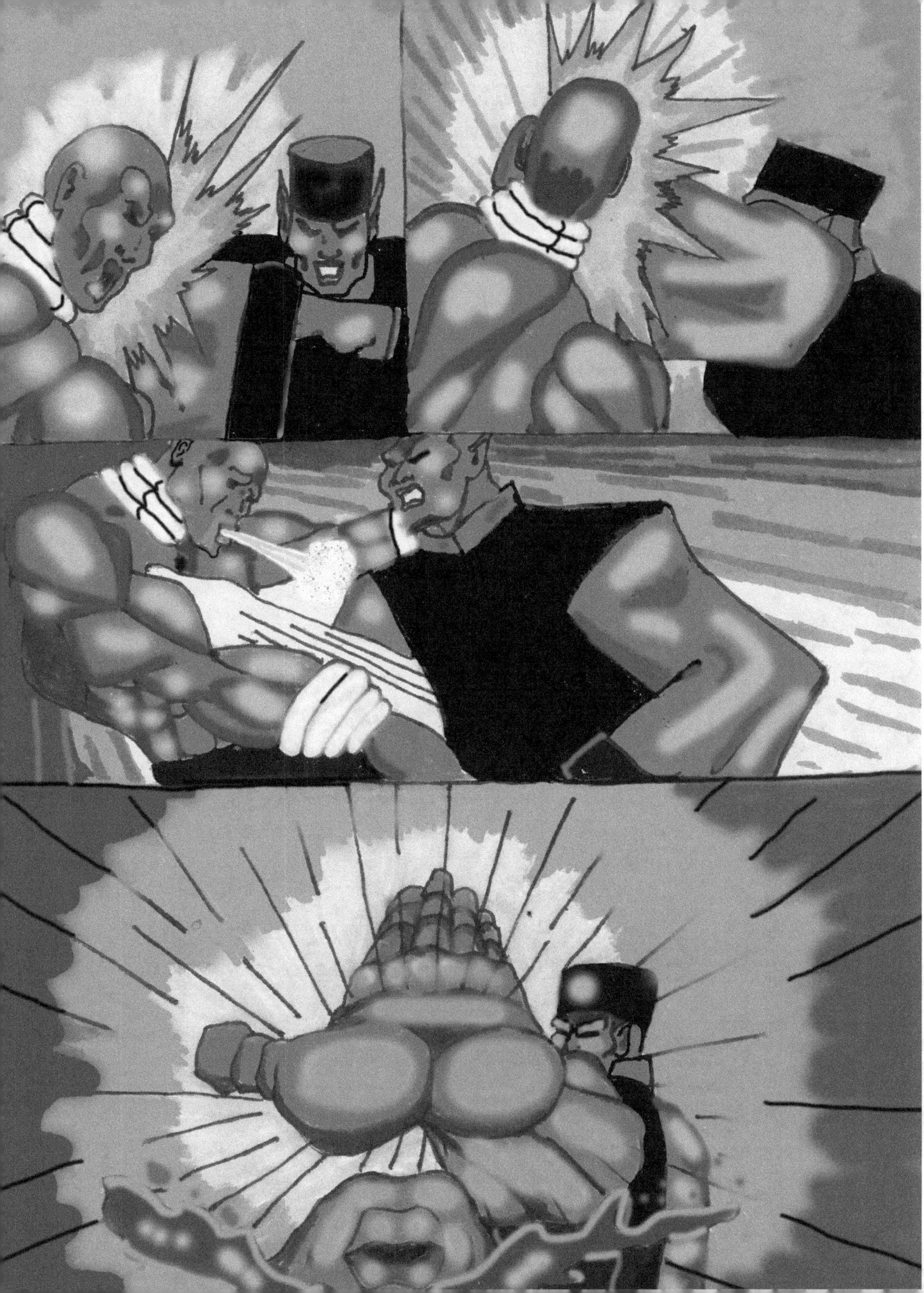

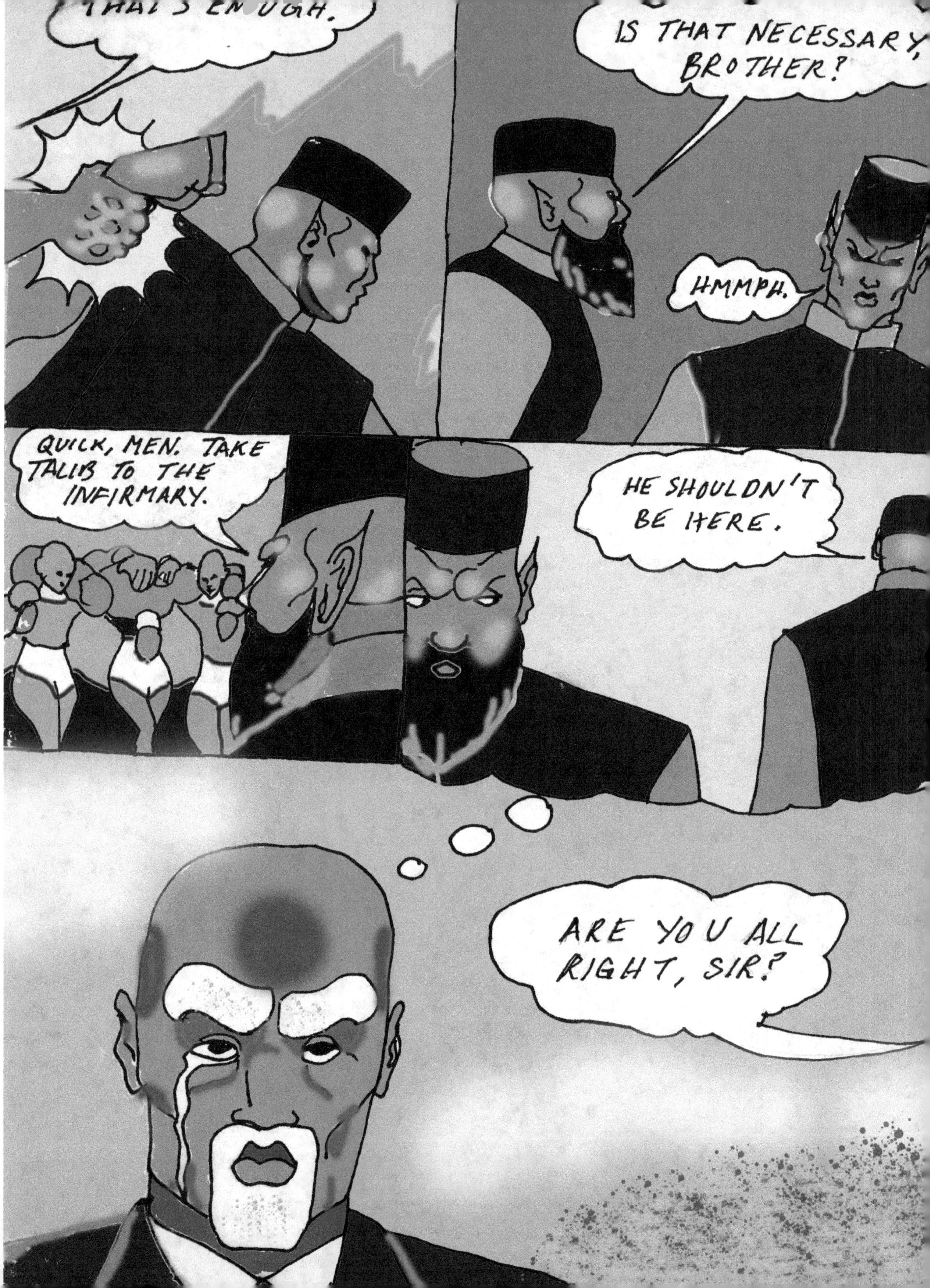
THAT'S ENOUGH.
IS THAT NECESSARY, BROTHER?
HMMPH.
QUICK, MEN. TAKE TALIB TO THE INFIRMARY.
HE SHOULDN'T BE HERE.
ARE YOU ALL RIGHT, SIR?

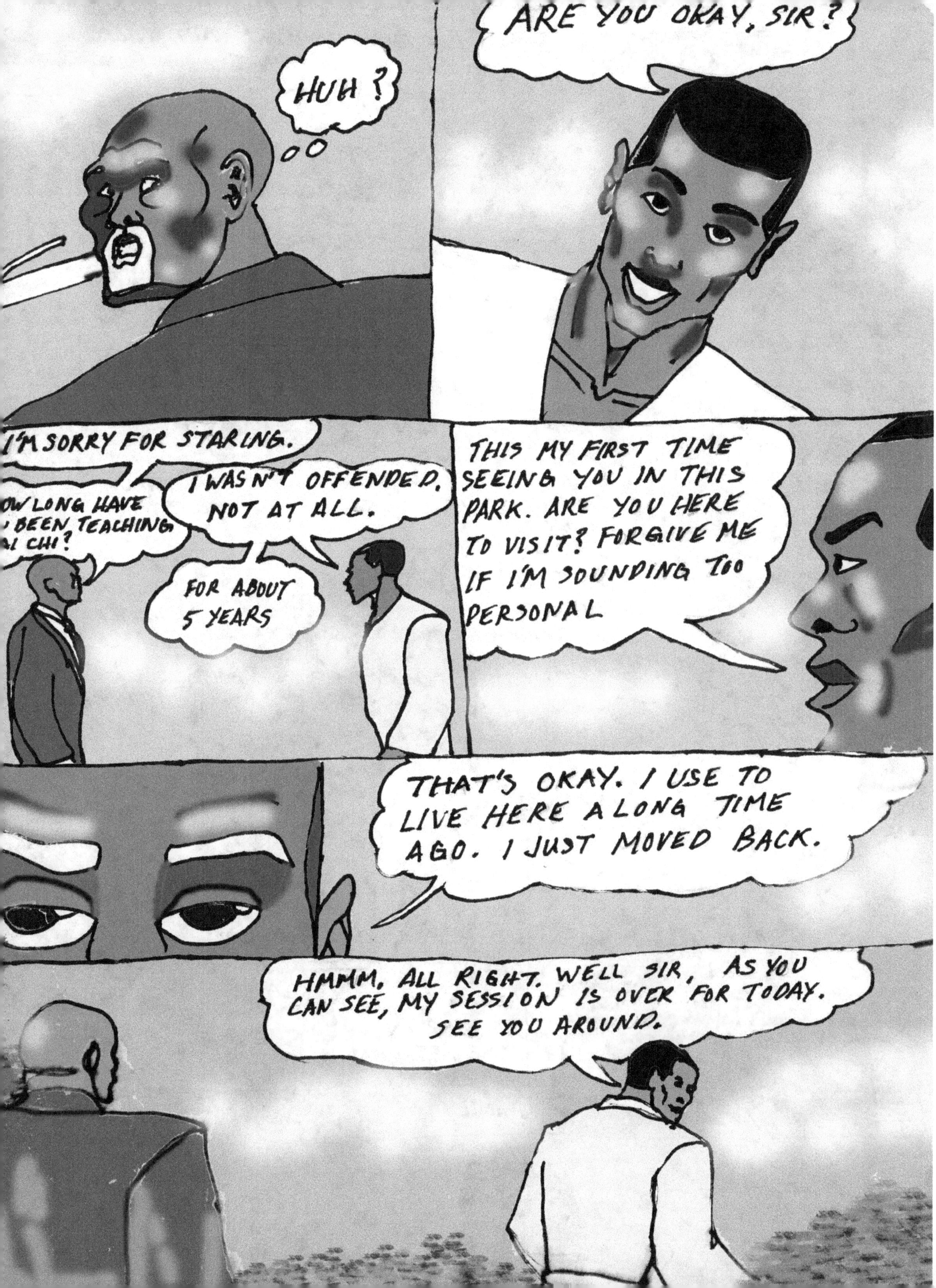
HUH ?
ARE YOU OKAY, SIR ?
I'M SORRY FOR STARING.
OW LONG HAVE
BEEN TEACHING
I CHI?
I WASN'T OFFENDED. NOT AT ALL.
FOR ABOUT 5 YEARS
THIS MY FIRST TIME SEEING YOU IN THIS PARK. ARE YOU HERE TO VISIT? FORGIVE ME IF I'M SOUNDING TOO PERSONAL
THAT'S OKAY. I USE TO LIVE HERE A LONG TIME AGO. I JUST MOVED BACK.
HMMM, ALL RIGHT. WELL SIR, AS YOU CAN SEE, MY SESSION IS OVER FOR TODAY. SEE YOU AROUND.

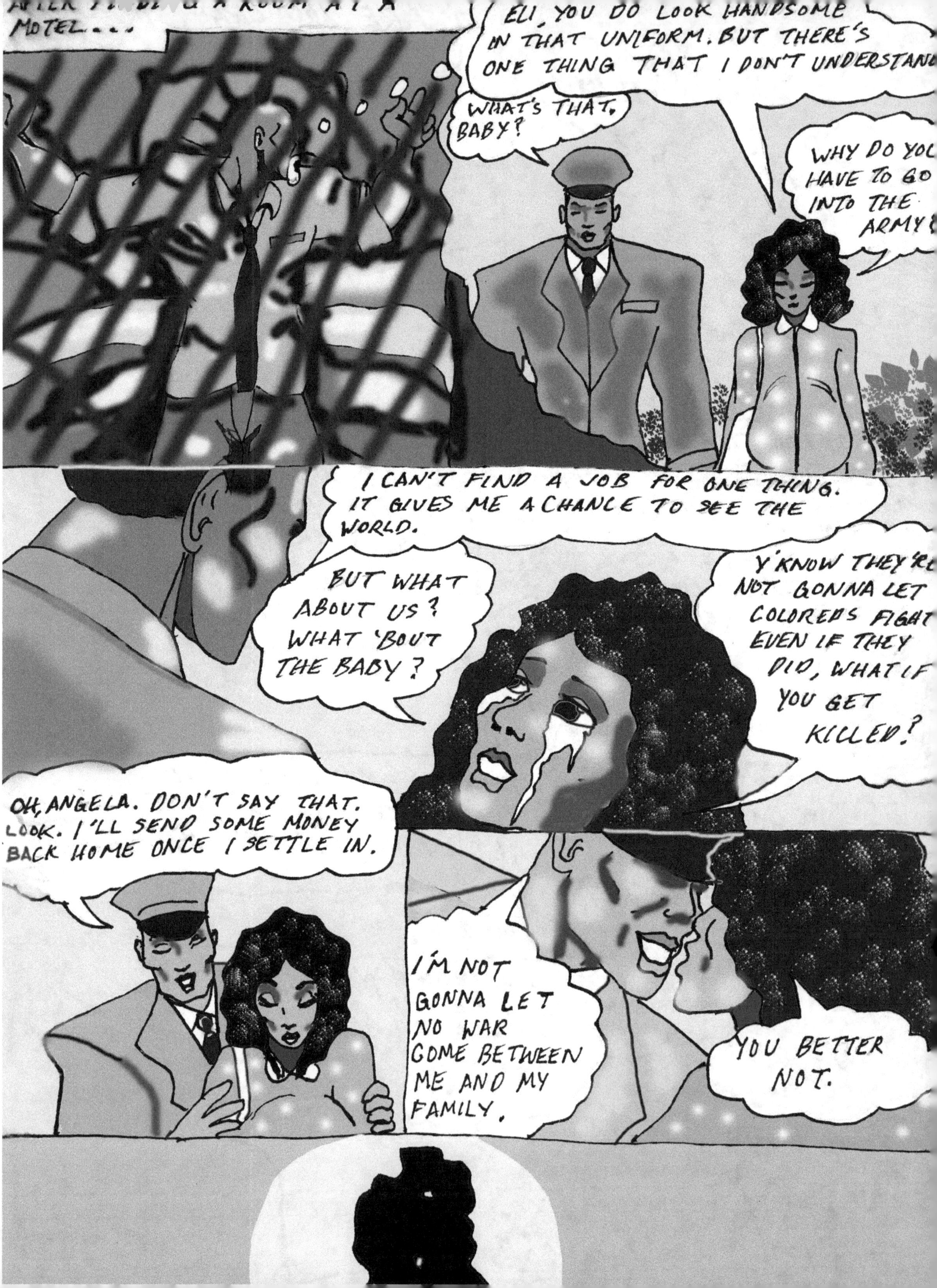
MOTEL...
ELI, YOU DO LOOK HANDSOME IN THAT UNIFORM. BUT THERE'S ONE THING THAT I DON'T UNDERSTAND
WHAT'S THAT, BABY?
WHY DO YOU HAVE TO GO INTO THE ARMY?
I CAN'T FIND A JOB FOR ONE THING. IT GIVES ME A CHANCE TO SEE THE WORLD.
BUT WHAT ABOUT US? WHAT 'BOUT THE BABY?
Y'KNOW THEY'RE NOT GONNA LET COLOREDS FIGHT EVEN IF THEY DID, WHAT IF YOU GET KILLED?
OH, ANGELA. DON'T SAY THAT. LOOK. I'LL SEND SOME MONEY BACK HOME ONCE I SETTLE IN.
I'M NOT GONNA LET NO WAR COME BETWEEN ME AND MY FAMILY.
YOU BETTER NOT.

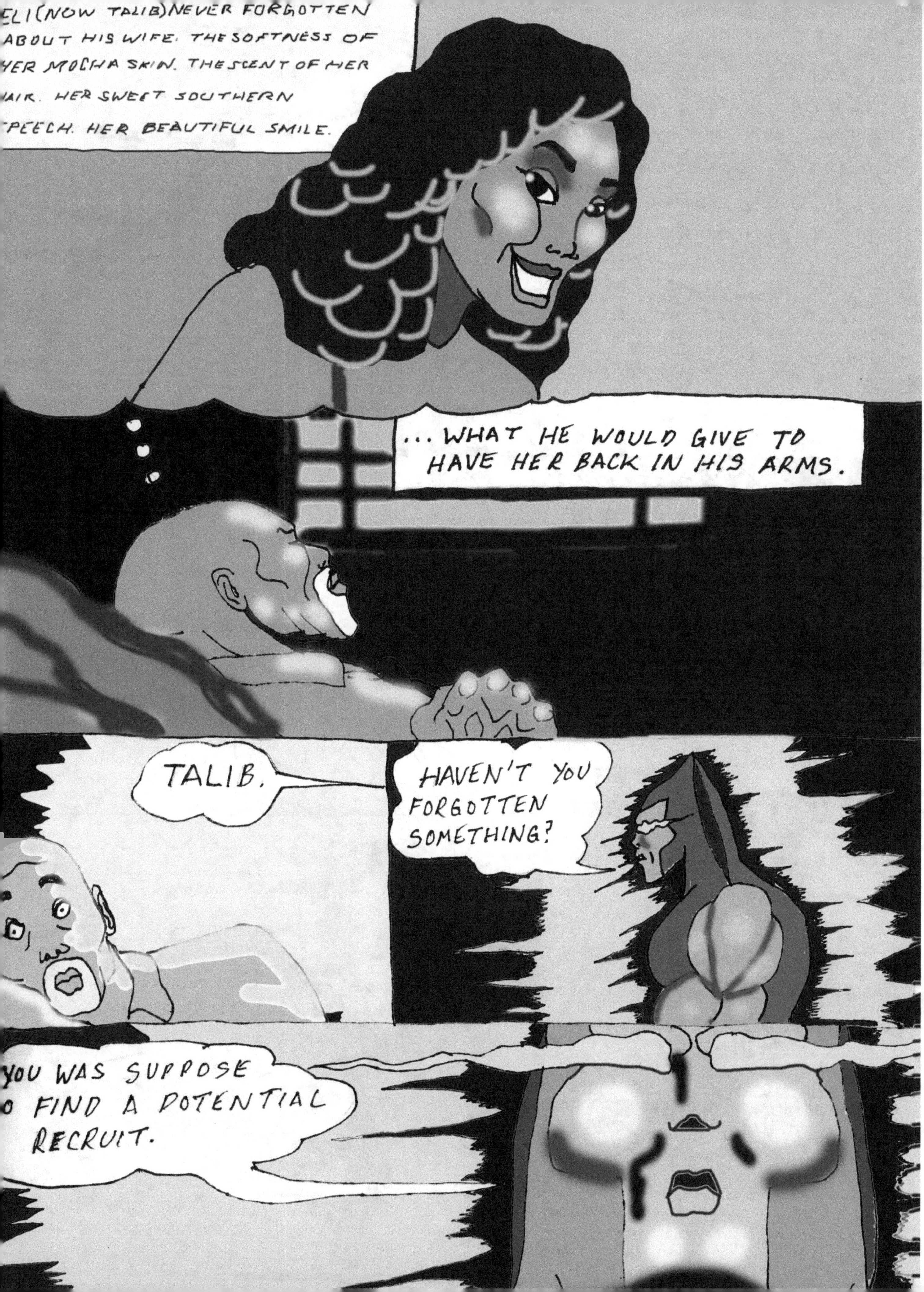
ELI(NOW TALIB)NEVER FORGOTTEN ABOUT HIS WIFE. THE SOFTNESS OF HER MOCHA SKIN. THE SCENT OF HER HAIR. HER SWEET SOUTHERN SPEECH. HER BEAUTIFUL SMILE.
...WHAT HE WOULD GIVE TO HAVE HER BACK IN HIS ARMS.
TALIB.
HAVEN'T YOU FORGOTTEN SOMETHING?
YOU WAS SUPPOSE TO FIND A POTENTIAL RECRUIT.

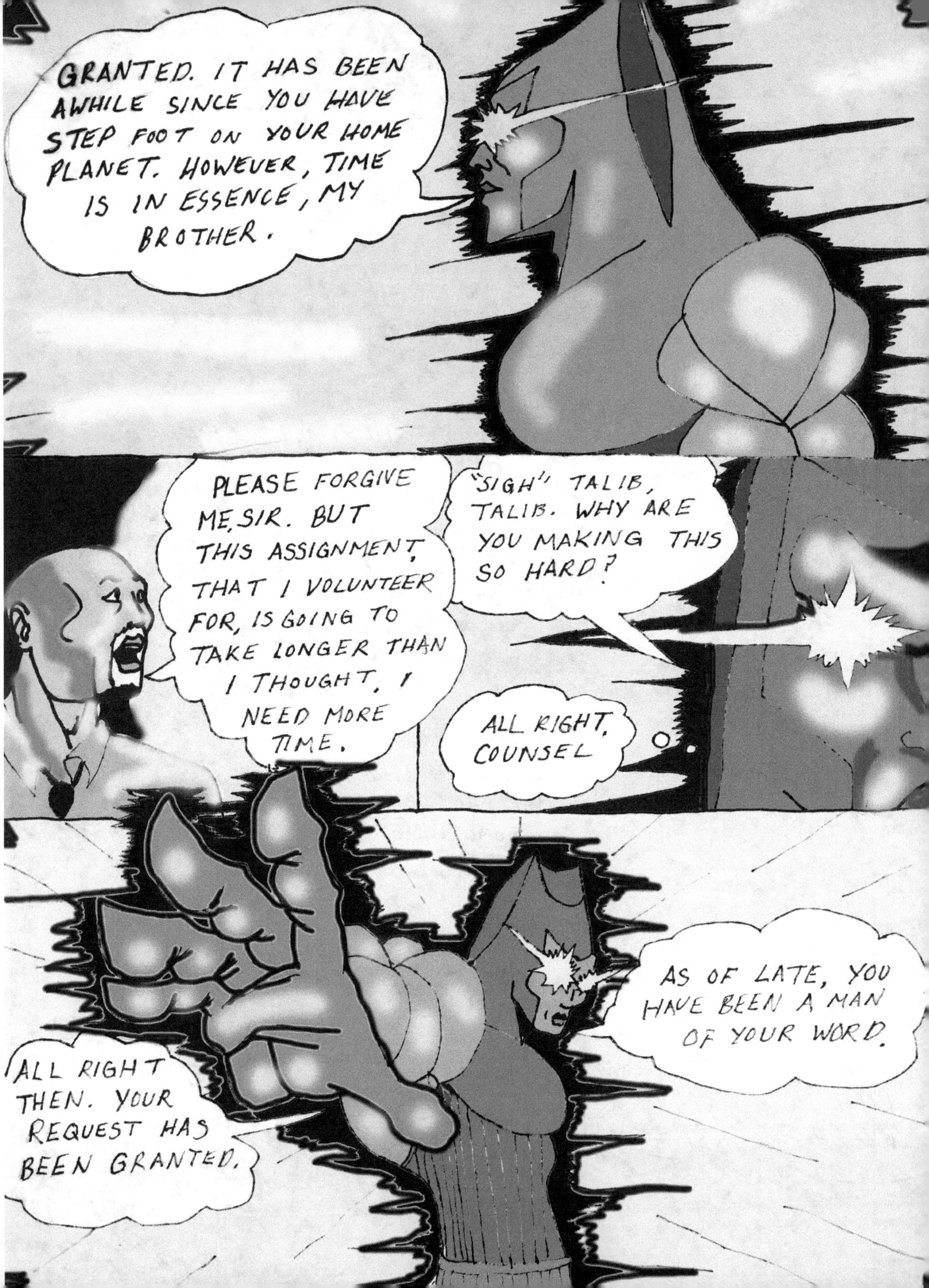
GRANTED. IT HAS BEEN AWHILE SINCE YOU HAVE STEP FOOT ON YOUR HOME PLANET. HOWEVER, TIME IS IN ESSENCE, MY BROTHER.
PLEASE FORGIVE ME, SIR. BUT THIS ASSIGNMENT, THAT I VOLUNTEER FOR, IS GOING TO TAKE LONGER THAN I THOUGHT. I NEED MORE TIME.
"SIGH" TALIB, TALIB. WHY ARE YOU MAKING THIS SO HARD?
ALL RIGHT, COUNSEL
AS OF LATE, YOU HAVE BEEN A MAN OF YOUR WORD.
ALL RIGHT THEN. YOUR REQUEST HAS BEEN GRANTED.

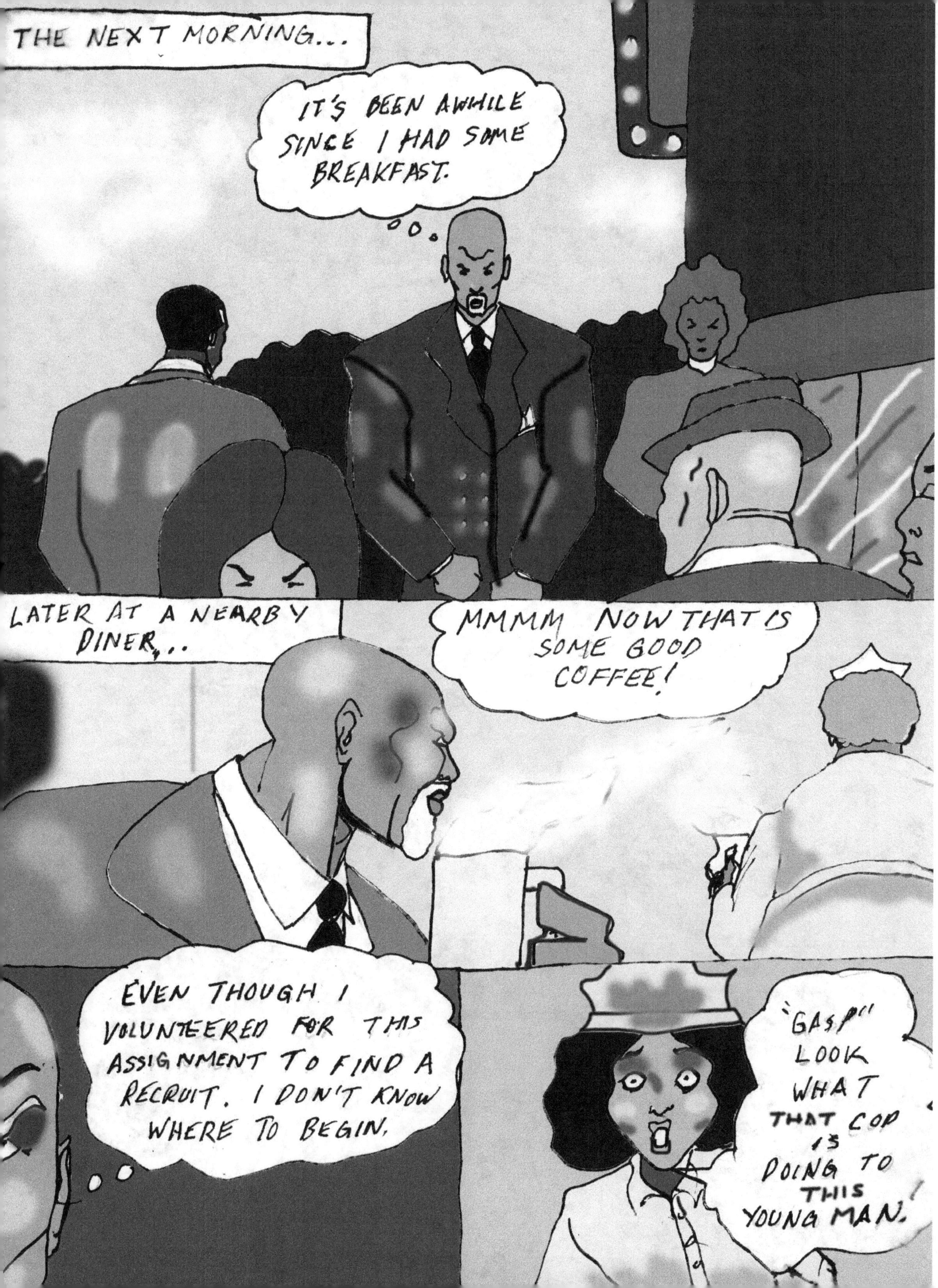
THE NEXT MORNING...
IT'S BEEN AWHILE SINCE I HAD SOME BREAKFAST.
LATER AT A NEARBY DINER...
MMMM NOW THAT IS SOME GOOD COFFEE!
EVEN THOUGH I VOLUNTEERED FOR THIS ASSIGNMENT TO FIND A RECRUIT. I DON'T KNOW WHERE TO BEGIN.
"GASP" LOOK WHAT THAT COP IS DOING TO THIS YOUNG MAN.

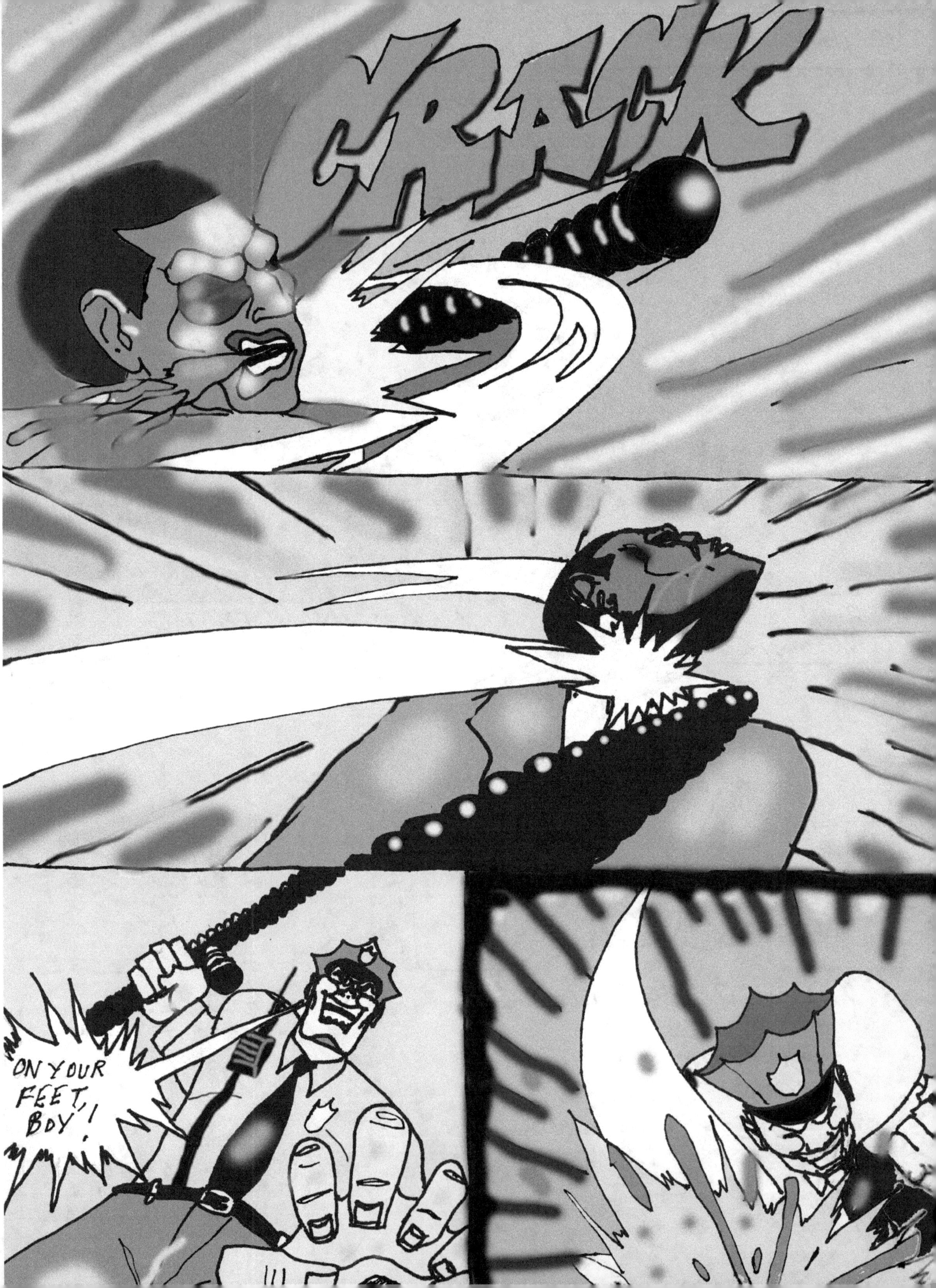
CRACK
ON YOUR FEET, BOY!

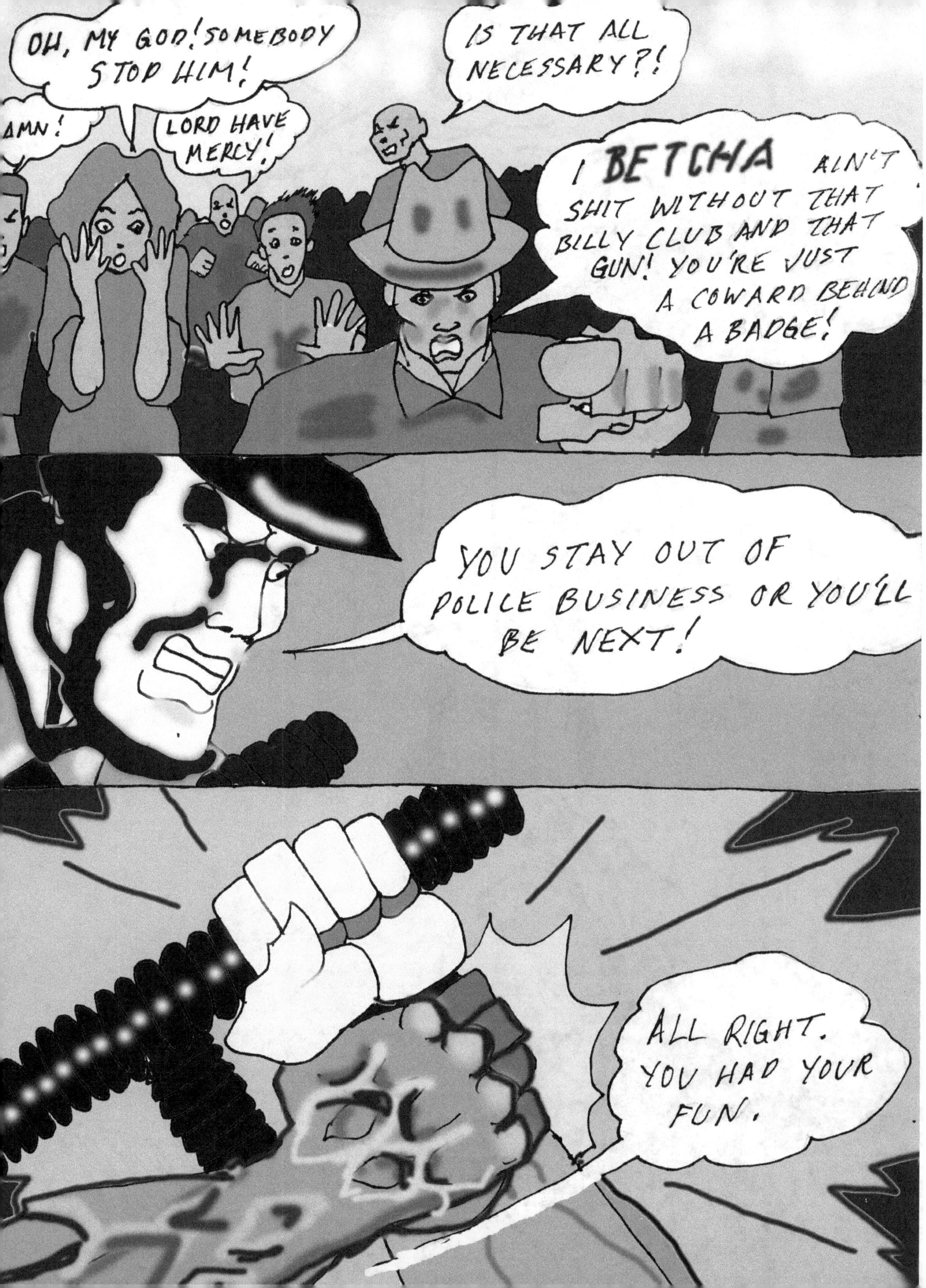

OH, MY GOD! SOMEBODY STOP HIM!
IS THAT ALL NECESSARY?!
AMN!
LORD HAVE MERCY!
I BETCHA AIN'T SHIT WITHOUT THAT BILLY CLUB AND THAT GUN! YOU'RE JUST A COWARD BEHIND A BADGE!
YOU STAY OUT OF POLICE BUSINESS OR YOU'LL BE NEXT!
ALL RIGHT. YOU HAD YOUR FUN.

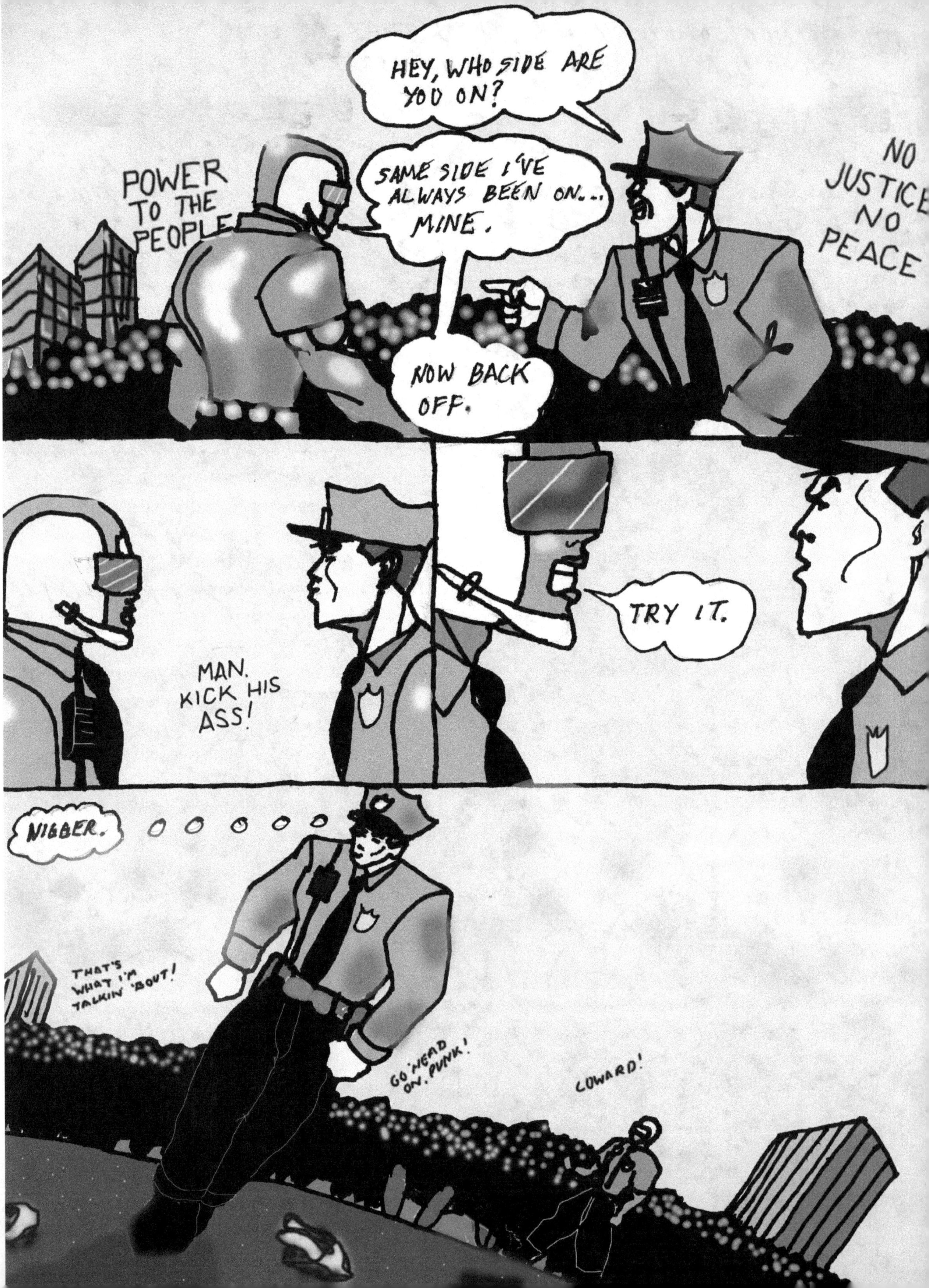
HEY, WHO SIDE ARE YOU ON?
POWER TO THE PEOPLE
NO JUSTICE NO PEACE
SAME SIDE I'VE ALWAYS BEEN ON... MINE.
NOW BACK OFF.
TRY IT.
MAN. KICK HIS ASS!
NIGGER.
THAT'S WHAT I'M TALKIN' 'BOUT!
GO 'HEAD ON, PUNK!
COWARD!

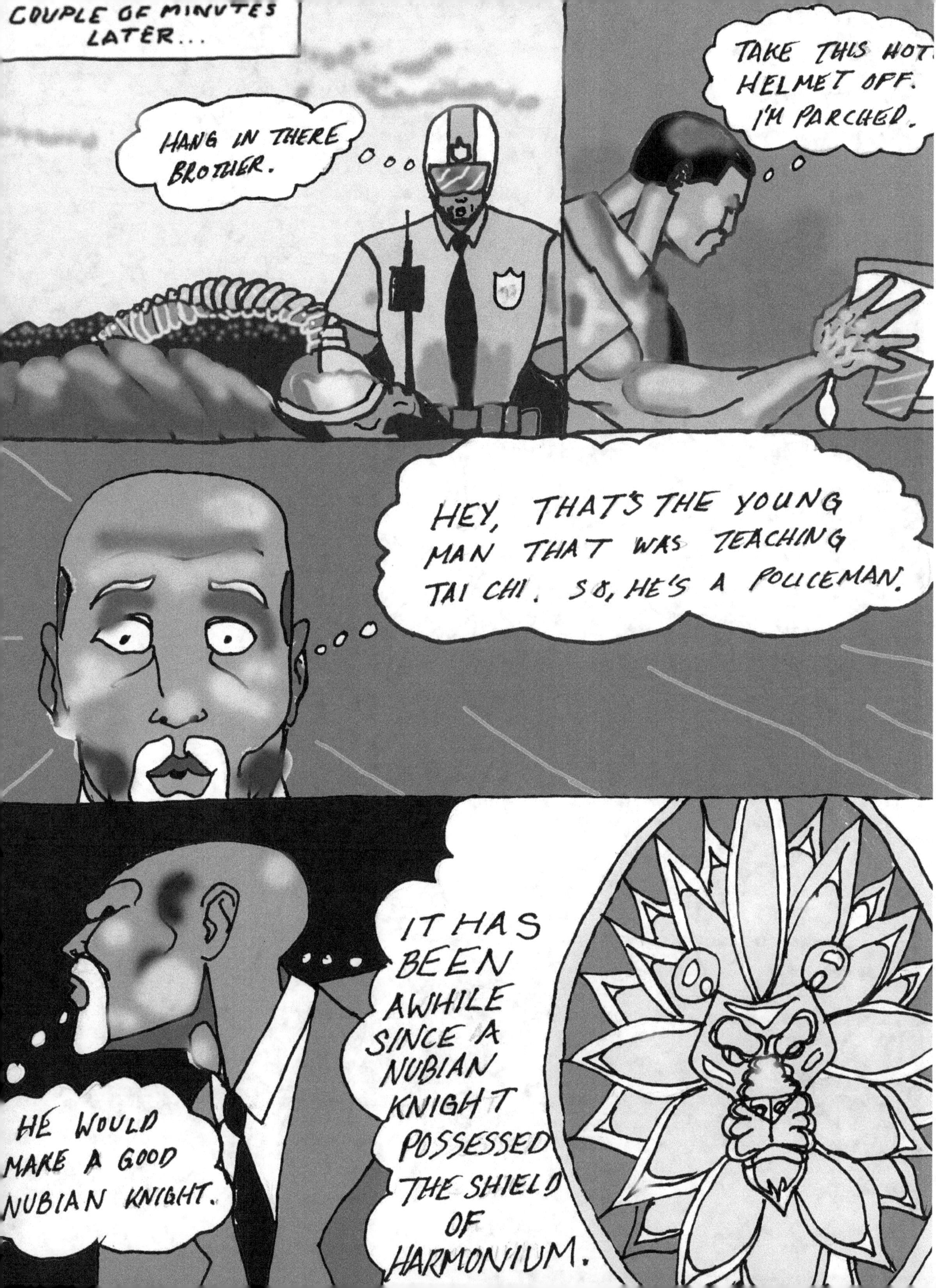
COUPLE OF MINUTES LATER...
HANG IN THERE BROTHER.
TAKE THIS HOT HELMET OFF. I'M PARCHED.
HEY, THAT'S THE YOUNG MAN THAT WAS TEACHING TAI CHI. SO, HE'S A POLICEMAN.
HE WOULD MAKE A GOOD NUBIAN KNIGHT.
IT HAS BEEN AWHILE SINCE A NUBIAN KNIGHT POSSESSED THE SHIELD OF HARMONIUM.

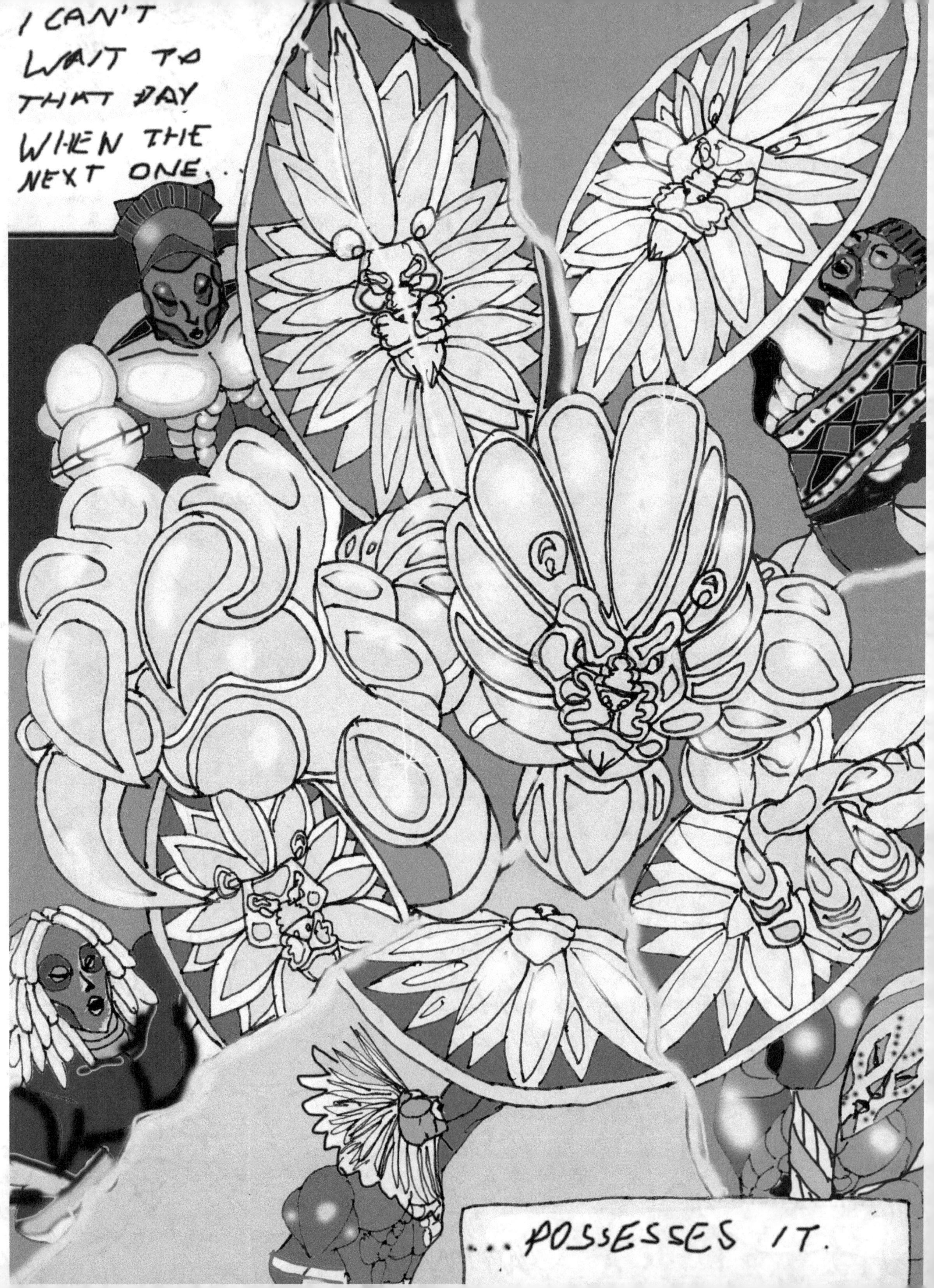
I CAN'T WAIT TO THAT DAY WHEN THE NEXT ONE...
...POSSESSES IT.

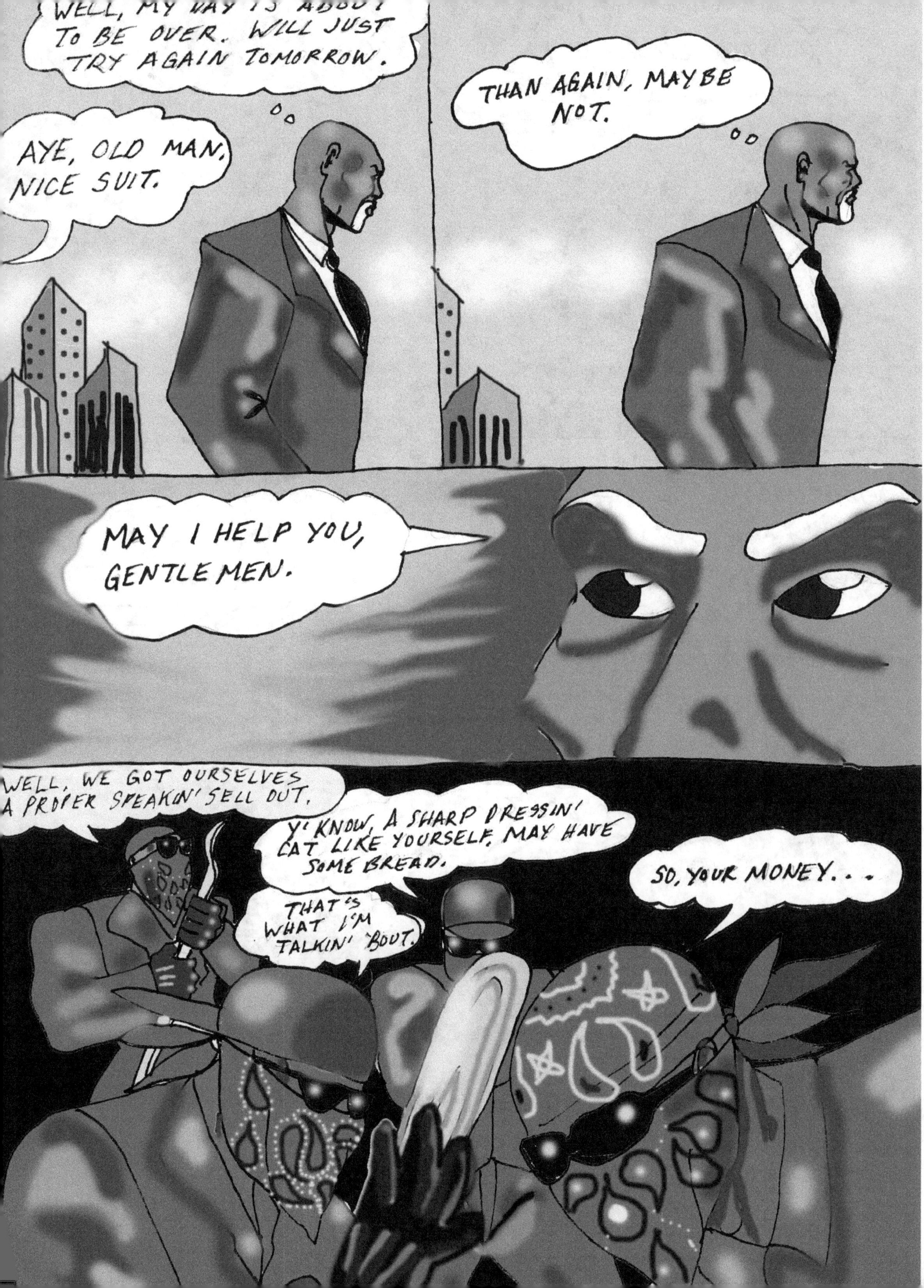
WELL, MY DAY IS ABOUT TO BE OVER. WILL JUST TRY AGAIN TOMORROW.
AYE, OLD MAN, NICE SUIT.
THAN AGAIN, MAYBE NOT.
MAY I HELP YOU, GENTLE MEN.
WELL, WE GOT OURSELVES A PROPER SPEAKIN' SELL OUT.
Y' KNOW, A SHARP DRESSIN' CAT LIKE YOURSELF, MAY HAVE SOME BREAD.
THAT'S WHAT I'M TALKIN' 'BOUT.
SO, YOUR MONEY...

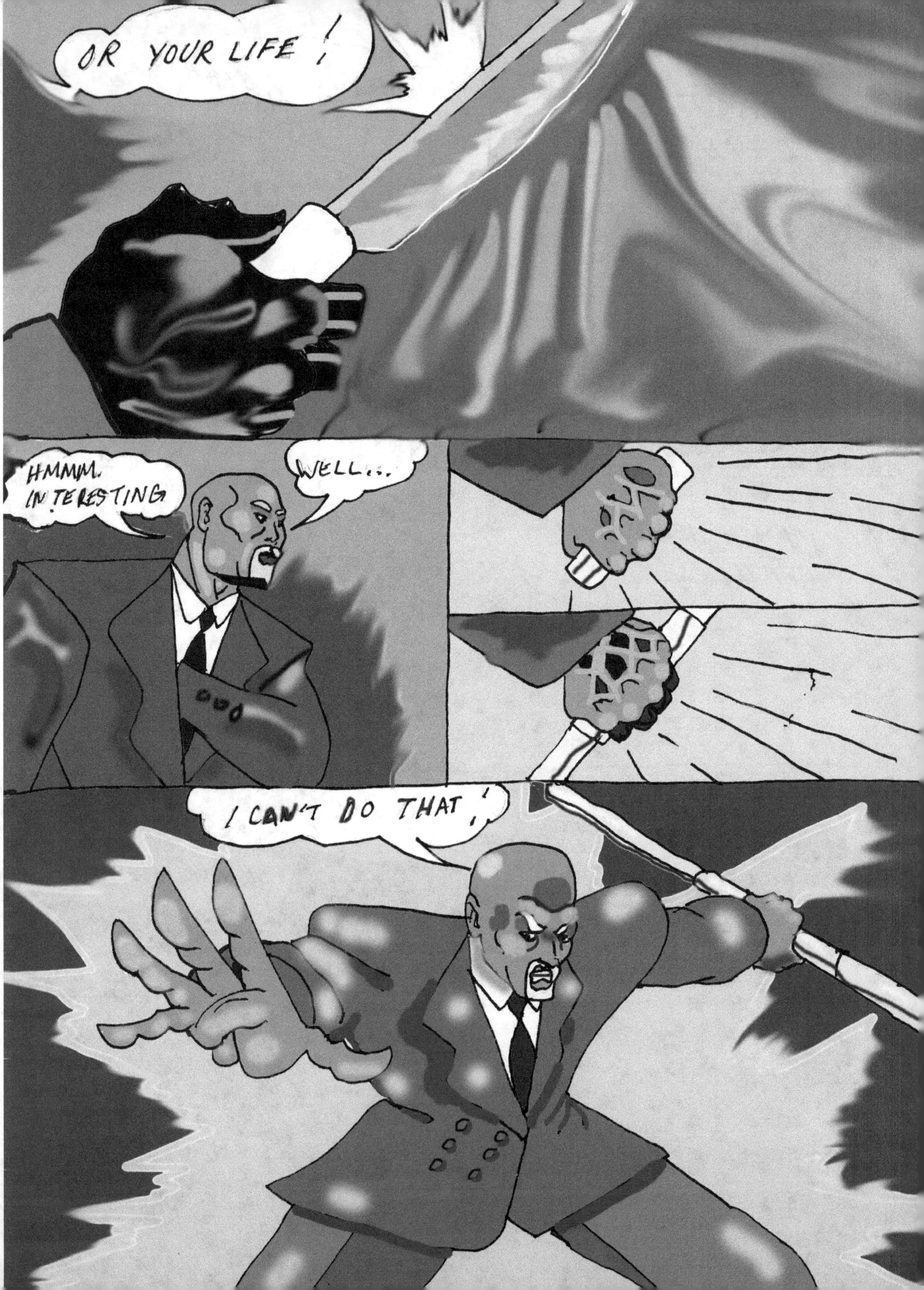
OR YOUR LIFE !
HMMM. INTERESTING
WELL...
I CAN'T DO THAT !

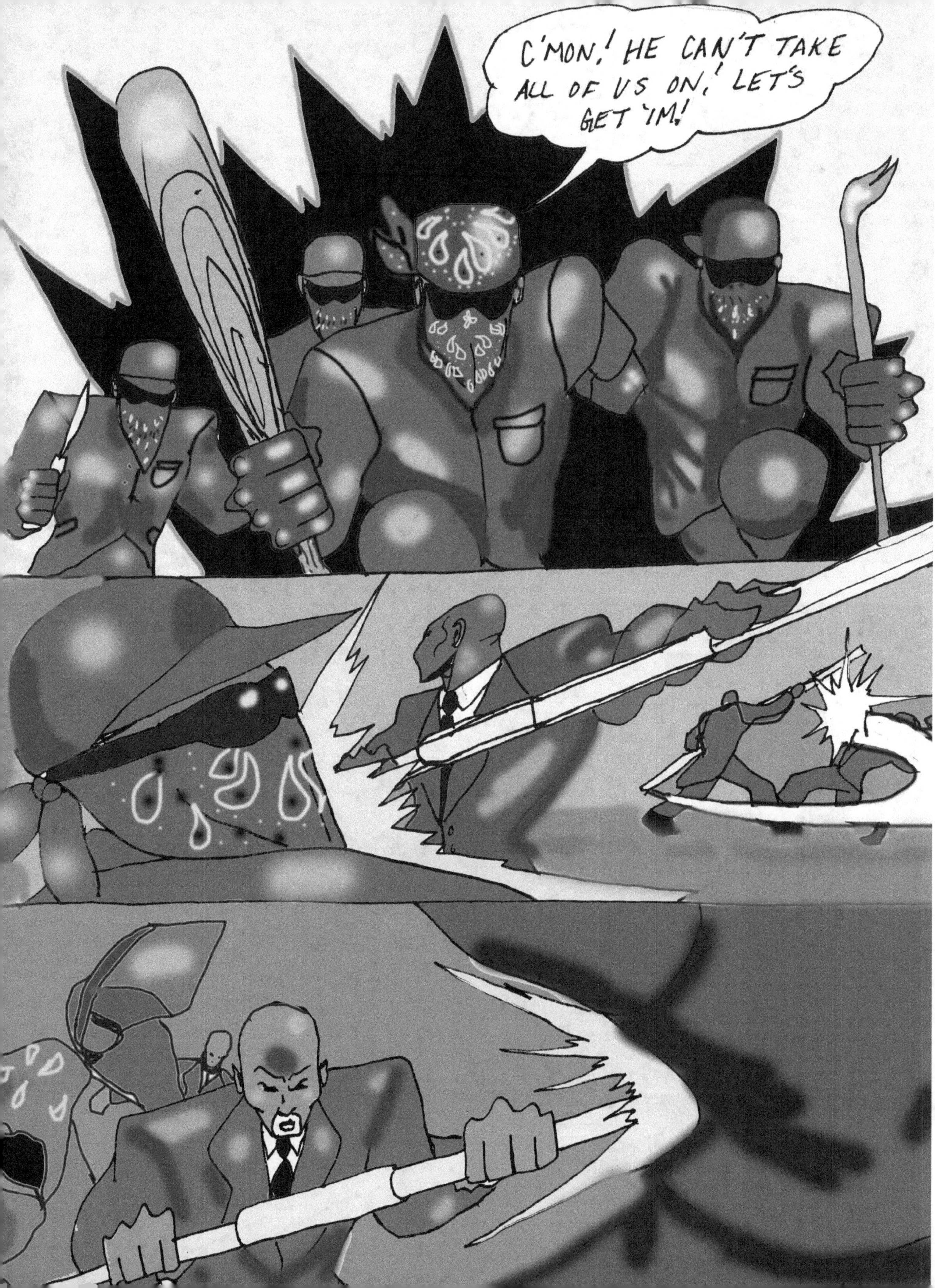
C'MON! HE CAN'T TAKE ALL OF US ON! LET'S GET 'IM!

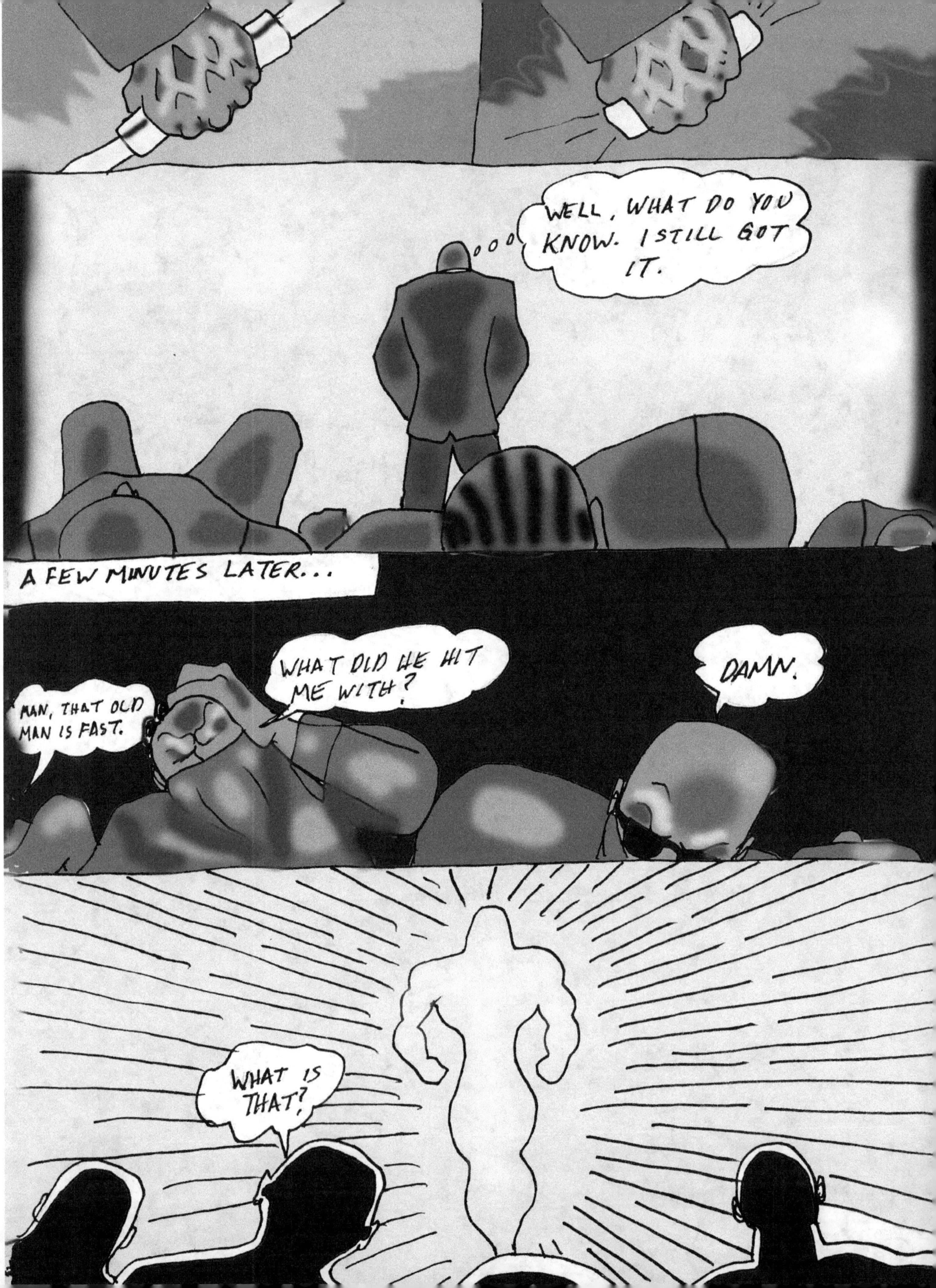
WELL, WHAT DO YOU KNOW. I STILL GOT IT.
A FEW MINUTES LATER...
MAN, THAT OLD MAN IS FAST.
WHAT DID HE HIT ME WITH?
DAMN.
WHAT IS THAT?

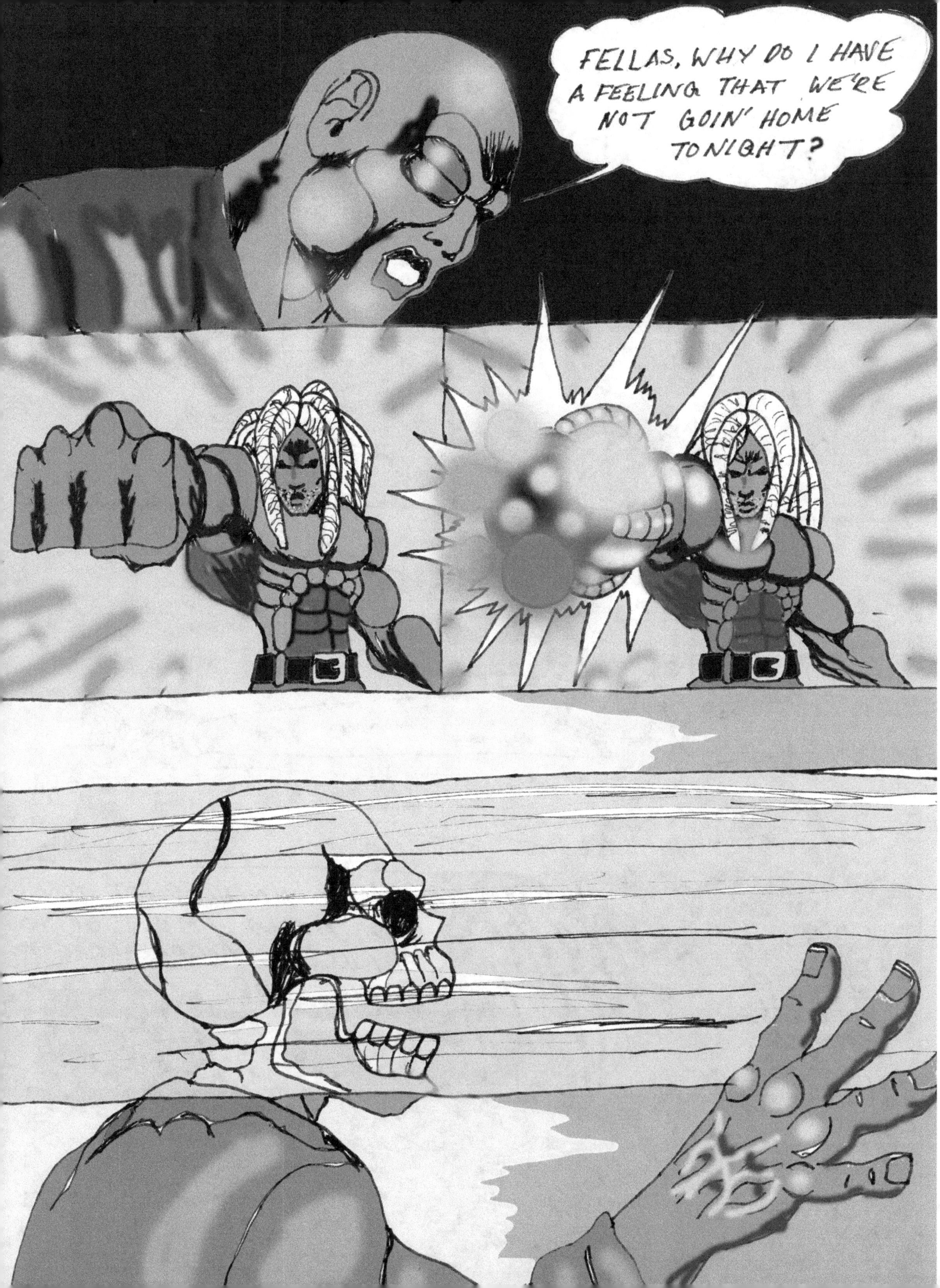
FELLAS, WHY DO I HAVE A FEELING THAT WE'RE NOT GOIN' HOME TONIGHT?

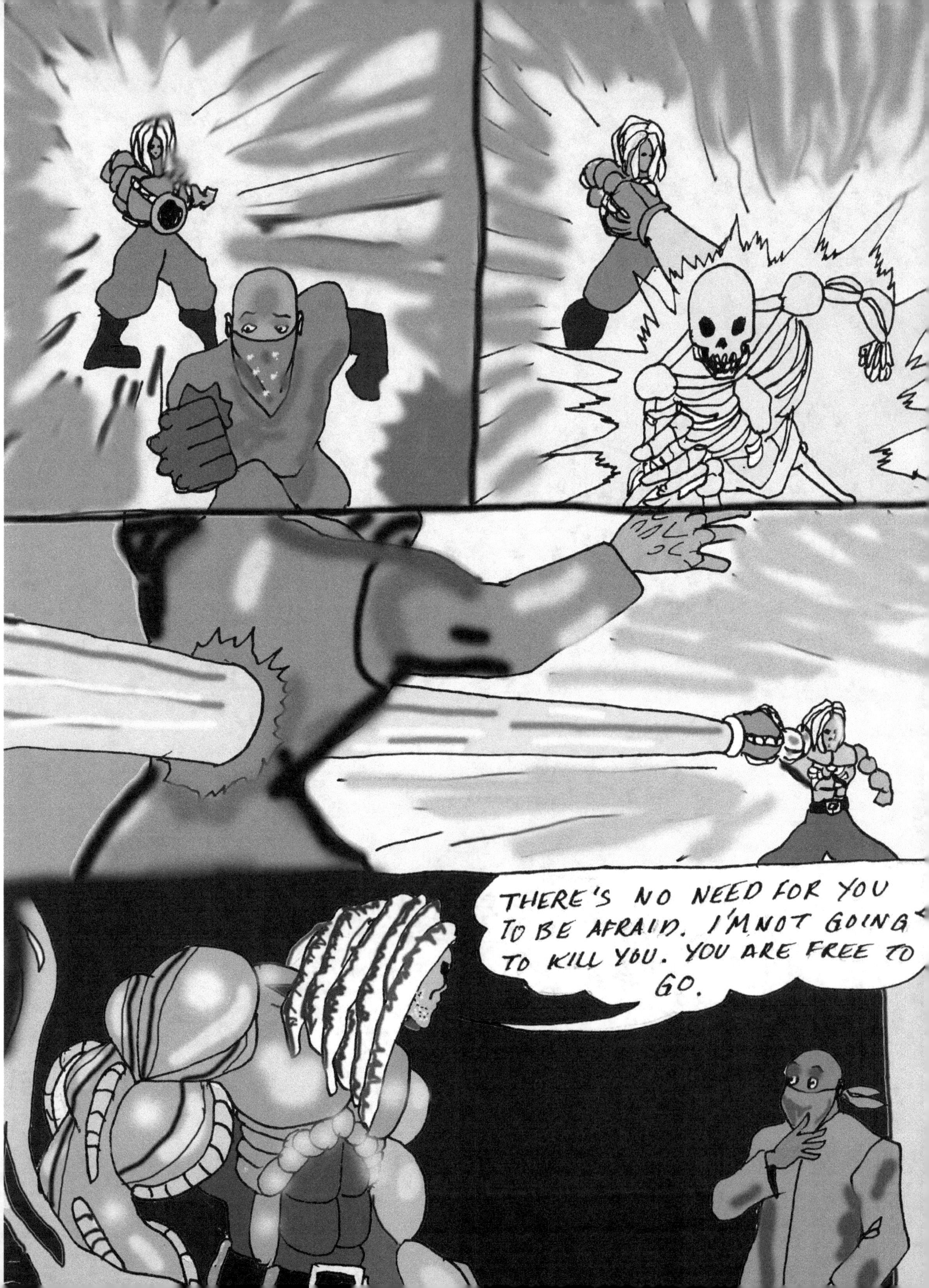
THERE'S NO NEED FOR YOU TO BE AFRAID. I'M NOT GOING TO KILL YOU. YOU ARE FREE TO GO.

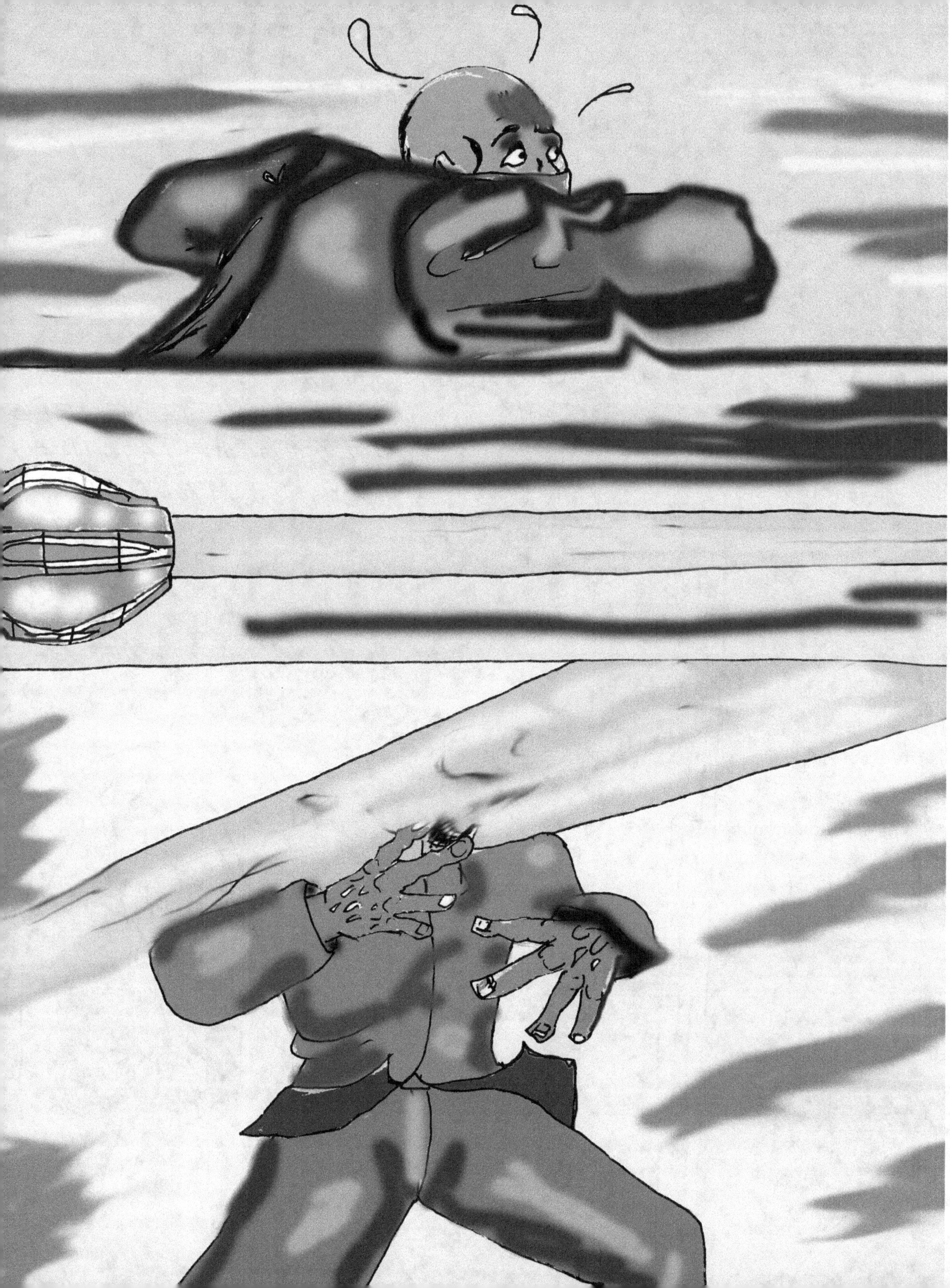

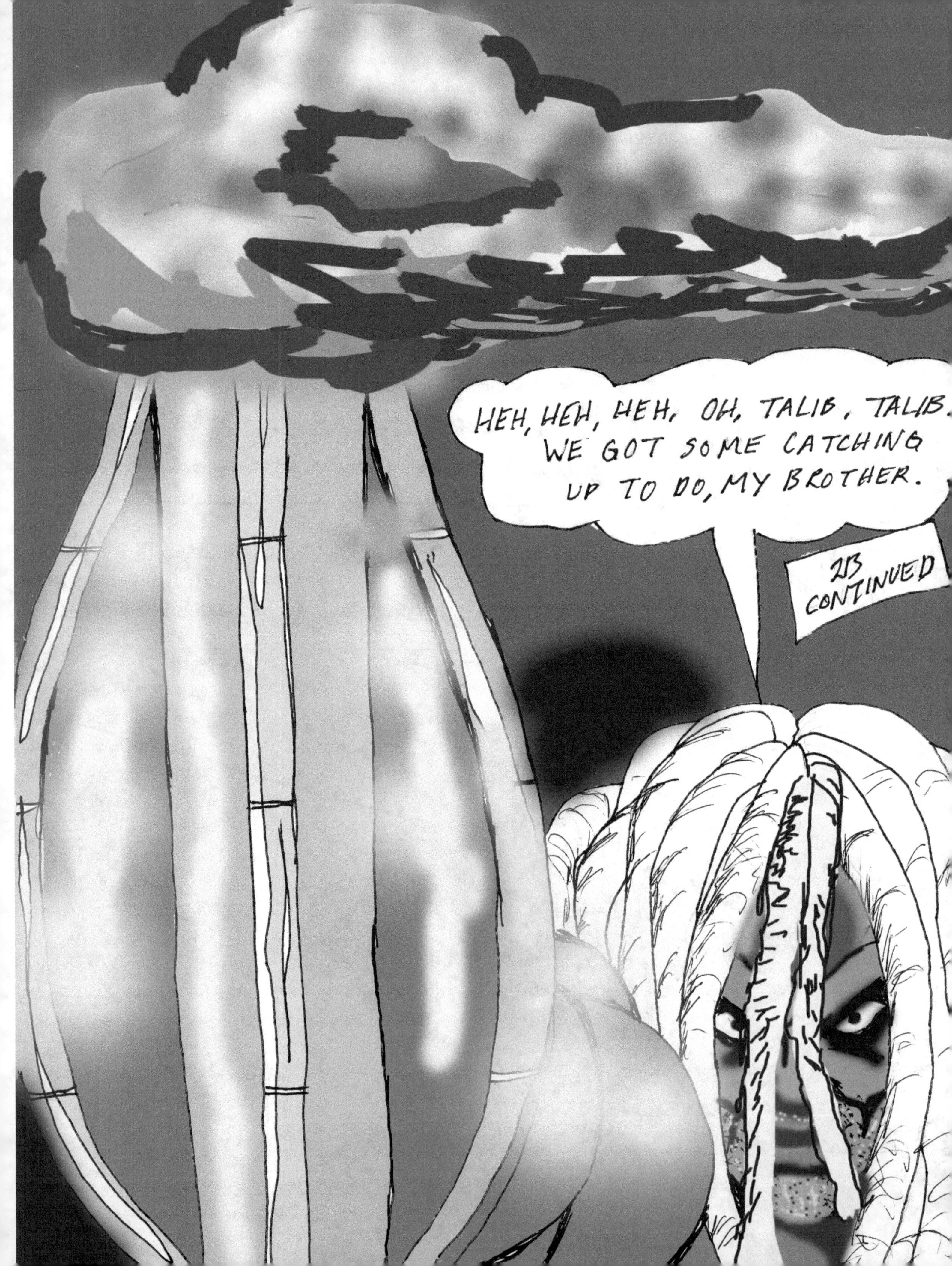
HEH, HEH, HEH, OH, TALIB, TALIB. WE GOT SOME CATCHING UP TO DO, MY BROTHER.
213 CONTINUED

www.ingramcontent.com/pod-product-compliance
Lightning Source LLC
Chambersburg PA
CBHW081314180526
45170CB00007B/2709
* 9 7 8 0 3 5 9 3 8 4 2 7 3 *